FLORIDA STATE
UNIVERSITY LIBRARIES

MAY 13 1999

TALLAHASSEE, FLORIDA

Women's Voices, Women's Rights

The Oxford Amnesty Lectures Series

Women's Voices, Women's Rights: Oxford Amnesty Lectures 1996,
edited by Alison Jeffries

FORTHCOMING

The Values of Science: Oxford Amnesty Lectures 1997,
edited by Wes Williams

Women's Voices, Women's Rights: Oxford Amnesty Lectures 1996

EDITED BY

Alison Jeffries

Westview Press
A Member of the Perseus Books Group

HQ
1236
.W655
1999

All rights reserved. Printed in the United States of America. No part of this publication may be reproduced or transmitted in any form or by any means, electronic or mechanical, including photocopy, recording, or any information storage and retrieval system, without permission in writing from the publisher.

Copyright © 1999 by Westview Press, A Member of the Perseus Books Group

Published in 1999 in the United States of America by Westview Press, 5500 Central Avenue, Boulder, Colorado 80301–2877, and in the United Kingdom by Westview Press, 12 Hid's Copse Road, Cumnor Hill, Oxford OX2 9JJ

Library of Congress Cataloging-in-Publication Data
Women's voices, women's rights : Oxford Amnesty lectures 1996 / edited by Alison Jeffries.
    p. cm.
Includes bibliographical references.
ISBN 0-8133-6876-6
  1. Women's rights. 2. Feminism. I. Jeffries, Alison.
HQ1236.W655   1999
305.42—dc21   98-23977
                                                                                                                      CIP

The paper used in this publication meets the requirements of the American National Standard for Permanence of Paper for Printed Library Materials Z39.48–1984.

10   9   8   7   6   5   4   3   2   1

Contents

Preface to the Oxford Amnesty Lectures vii
Acknowledgments ix

Introduction, *Alison Jeffries* 1

1 The Feminist Critique of Liberalism, *Martha Nussbaum* 13

2 Women's Rights: Whose Obligations? *Onora O'Neill* 57

3 Are Women Human? *Marilyn French* 71

4 "Women Are Like Cold Mutton": Power, Humiliation, and a New Definition of Human Rights, *Naomi Wolf* 93

5 Each Man in His Cave, *Michèle le Doeuff* 101

6 Women's Rights in Today's Political Climate, *Shere Hite with responses by Alison Jeffries and Sarah Ansari* 117

About the Editor and Contributors 135

Preface to the Oxford Amnesty Lectures

A single idea governs the Oxford Amnesty Lectures. Speakers of international reputation are invited to lecture in Oxford on a subject related to human rights. The public is charged to hear them. In this way funds are raised for Amnesty International, and the profile of human rights is raised in the academic and the wider communities.

The organization of the lectures is the work of a group of Amnesty supporters. They act with the approval of Amnesty International but are independent of it. Neither the themes of the annual series nor the views expressed by the speakers should be confused with the views of Amnesty itself. For each annual series a general theme is proposed, bringing a particular discipline or perspective to bear on human rights. The speakers are invited to submit an unpublished lecture, which is delivered in Oxford; the lectures are then published as a book.

Amnesty International is a worldwide voluntary movement that works to prevent some of the gravest violations by governments of people's fundamental human rights. Its 1.1 million members campaign to *free all prisoners of conscience* (these are people detained anywhere for their beliefs or because of their ethnic origin, sex, color, or language—who have not used or advocated violence); *ensure fair and prompt trials for all political prisoners; abolish the death penalty, torture, and other cruel treatment of prisoners; end extrajudicial executions and "disappearances."* Amnesty International also opposes abuses by opposition groups: hostage taking, torture, and killing of prisoners and other arbitrary killings. Amnesty International, recognizing that human rights are indivisible and interdependent, works to promote all the human rights enshrined in the Universal Declaration of Human Rights and other international standards, through human rights education programs and campaigning for the ratification of human rights treaties. Amnesty International is impartial: It is independent of any government, political persuasion, or religious creed. It does not support or oppose any government or political system, nor does it support or oppose views of the victims whose rights it seeks to protect. It is concerned solely with the protection of the human rights involved in each case, regardless of the ideology of the government, opposition forces, or the beliefs of the victim.

Members of the Committee of the Oxford Amnesty Lectures 1996 were Madeleine Forey, John Gardner, Wes Williams, Fabienne Pagnier, and Stephen Shute.

Alison Jeffries

Acknowledgments

I would like to thank the Committee of the Oxford Amnesty Lectures for inviting me to edit this volume. I am grateful to Chris Miller and Madeleine Forey for reading drafts and for their encouragement throughout. I owe much to my husband, Terry Hoad, for his patient reading of successive drafts of the introduction and of the comments on the final lecture. Without his help and support, and without the patience of Nicholas and Abigail, this volume would not have been completed.

A. J.

Introduction

Alison Jeffries

The title of this volume, *Women's Voices, Women's Rights*, might be taken innocently to indicate its contents: a set of lectures given by women on the rights of women, on the failure to achieve those rights, and on the reasons and remedies for those failures. However, it might also imply that women's rights are not simply the extension of the agreed rights of men to all members of the community but that, as Michèle le Doeuff suggests in her lecture, to experience is to know. In other words, the "lived in" experience of being female results in a distinctive account of the nature of rights and the applicability of the language of rights to the status of women as equally valuable social, political, and economic agents. Women, therefore, might be expected to give a distinctive critique of the theory of rights that depends on their difference from men.

That seemingly simple couplet thus disguises a wealth of methodological and theoretical debate that goes to the heart of feminist analysis, and it takes us with feminists and others to the site of some of the richest critique of the liberal political theory that has driven the human rights movement. In line with the two possible readings of the volume's title, some of the criticism contained in the lectures is internal, located in the incoherence that focusing on the experience of women lays bare. Other criticisms are more far-reaching, suggesting that if the language of rights is to have significance for women, it must move beyond the liberal theoretical framework that engendered it. Always, however, the criticisms rest on a shared commitment to the dignity, humanity, and unique individuality of each human person—a tenet that underpins the human rights movement, provides the moral impetus for feminism, and, indeed, is the motive force behind Amnesty International's campaigning on behalf of political prisoners worldwide.

Of the debates that we have already opened, the first concerns the alternative methodological stances that women have applied to the analysis of their status, that is, to the competing approaches to be found within feminist analysis. Is to speak in a woman's voice to speak, in Carol Gilligan's famous phrase, "in different voice?"[1] The debate between "equality" and "difference" feminism has been raging now for more than fifteen years and is to some extent burning out. Gilligan's particular empirical claim—that abstract moral reasoning based on principles of justice is a specifically male faculty, while women's moral reasoning reflects their more immediate grounding in relationships and caring roles—has been subjected to far-reaching criticism on empirical and philosophical grounds. However, a powerful strand of feminism remains wedded to the wider claim that the life cycle and moral development of women, particularly in the experience of motherhood, means that moral and ethical reasoning designed by and for men does not make sense of the lives or the moral principles of women.[2] Such a claim leads to a suspicion that the universalized and abstract language of rights will always and necessarily fail to ensure the conditions in which women can enjoy individual dignity and respect. The very methodology of rights theory will ensure women's exclusion.

None of the authors in this volume has adopted this "separatist" approach in any simple way, but the influence of the debate is, nevertheless, pervasive. Nussbaum and O'Neill specifically situate their work with reference to that debate, attempting to answer some of its challenges. French, Wolf, and le Doeuff make use of insights about the "difference" of women to give purchase to their arguments about the weakness of the discourse of rights with respect to women.

The authors in this volume might also be helpfully situated with respect to the older categories applied to feminist thought: the distinctions between liberal, radical, and socialist feminism.[3] Liberal feminism, represented here by Martha Nussbaum and Onora O'Neill, seeks to use liberal theory to undermine institutions and practices that systematically discriminate against women. It also addresses weaknesses in liberal theory that are demonstrated by the application of that theory to the lives and experiences of women.

It has often been observed that the difference between radical and socialist feminism seems to depend largely on the side of the Atlantic on which one is writing. Both groups, however, criticize liberal feminists for their inadequate account of the social and economic sources of power that sustain inequalities between women and men. In this volume Marilyn French offers a classic radical feminist account of the development of masculinity in contemporary societies. Unless one addresses the sources of this power in the most intimate realms of the family and of sexuality, one will not succeed in the attempt to grant women human rights. Naomi Wolf too tries to uncover what she calls the social and anthropological workings of the power relationships of men over women in the denial of sexual dignity to women. She argues, effectively, that formal equality granted in law will not address the problem of female inequality. Both Wolf and French make implicit use of the 1960s radical feminist slogan "the personal is political." That is to say, any attempt to sustain a sharp distinction between the public and private spheres of life will tend to cover over sources of male power, and of female powerlessness, that ensure that women remain second class citizens.

Michèle le Doeuff also works on the sources of female oppression in the private sphere, in this case in the sphere of marriage. However, her work is not properly understood as a work of "radical feminism": rather it should be situated in the somewhat different context of the social and political thought that helped to shape French feminist theory. This approach has been greatly influenced by insights from psychoanalysis and from interpretive theory. Le Doeuff's paper shows these influences in its account of the construction of male power and sexuality through the particular configuration of the institution of marriage, which itself derives from the state's desire to promulgate a high birthrate.

In all feminist approaches, however, what is constant is the engagement of political theory with empirical reality. The political project of feminism requires that theoretical reflection on status and rights be tested in observations of the lives of women. As such, feminist theory has the capacity to subvert the deceptive simplicity of abstract reason, and also to demonstrate the complexity that any theoretical approach must encompass if it is to make adequate sense of experience. One consequence of this engagement is that writers from different methodological schools are engaged with the same substantive problems, so that there is significant crossover and interaction between approaches. In the present volume, for example, Hite appeals for a proper assertion of liberal values in terms that seem close to those of radical feminism in its analysis of male power and female sexual oppression. Several of the authors refer to the impact of economic markets on the structure of the family and the situation of women in the public sphere, an insight typically attributed to socialist feminism. Any sharp distinction between feminist approaches thus quickly breaks down. The attempt to situate the authors in this collection within the terms of feminist debate, therefore, should be taken as an indication of the likely resonances of the arguments that each employs rather than as an attempt at a rigid taxonomy.

One particular example of the cross-fertilization of feminist approaches leads us on to a wider challenge posed by the lectures collected here. Nussbaum, in common with liberal feminists such as Susan Moller Okin,[4] accepts that aspects of the private sphere must be subjected to the demands of a liberal theory of justice if women are to be the full bearers of rights. From a quite different perspective Michèle le Doeuff criticizes the privileged status of relations within the family, expressing disquiet at the way in which documents such as the European Convention on Human Rights entrench a right to the privacy of family life. While seemingly straightforward, however, this shared insight opens a realm of difficulty. For classical liberals the most evident problem is that to license the state to intervene in intimate personal relationships might be seen to risk dismantling a significant barrier to totalitarianism. Individual freedom might be taken to be predicated on a gap between the sphere of law and the sphere of private choice and personal autonomy.

Feminists might reasonably reply, with O'Neill, that such a gap has long since ceased to exist in modern "welfare" states, with on the one hand state regulation of marriage, divorce, child rearing, education and so on, and on the other the complex interaction between private individuals and the state as provider of welfare and other services. In that sense, one might well imagine an attempt to ensure that the laws governing these interactions should be subjected to the demands of liberal justice, without thereby countenancing intrusive intervention into the lives of individuals. However, a further problem is raised by the idea that certain social practices are not compatible with the "rights" of women. This is the issue of "culture," and the claim that to insist on ruling out certain forms of organization of private life—forms sanctioned by traditional, and often by religious, practice—is to open oneself to the charge of cultural imperialism. This criticism is one instantiation of the wider claim that the generalization of any theory about human dignity and status tends to impose the norms of the members of one culture on others who do not share the same perspective. Hence it is a difficulty that feminist theory shares with theories of the universal applicability of claims of human rights, and so it is of particular note in the context of a book seeking to explore aspects of the theory of human rights in the light of the work of Amnesty International.

This is, however, an especially biting criticism for feminist theory. In the last twenty years a fierce argument has raged about the way in which the concerns of white, middle-class women have been presented as applicable to all women.[5] Feminists have struggled not just with differences between women and men but with differences between women, on the grounds of class, race, sexuality, and ethnic culture. Some black women, for example, have argued that instead of being a sphere of oppression the family is the source of strength in a racist society. Interestingly, this mirrors le Doeuff's suggestion that marriage takes on a different quality in situations of the shared oppression of men and women. This argument about the possibility of a single feminist analysis has taken place within the context of a given society, for example, Britain or the United States. How much more problematic, therefore, is the application of any particular feminist analysis to other societies, especially where women are often implicated in what appears to us to be the oppression of other women.[6]

Unsurprisingly, in the light of this complexity, many feminists have moved further to embrace the wider challenge posed by postmodernism to the notion of the unified subject, and in consequence to any universal theory of rights. Ultimately, postmodernism might question whether even the notion of "woman," and thus of a woman's voice, is meaningful. This is not the place to rehearse the complex arguments surrounding this body of theory, except to ask whether we are thereby bound to abandon any attempt to criticize our own or any society from the perspective of women. To put this another way, is listening to "women's voices" on the subject of "women's rights" necessarily a meaningless endeavor?

One possibility at this point would be simply to reject the line of reasoning that leads to this uncertainty in the assertion of values, and to insist on a single, abstractly derived, set of principles that describe a just society. However, this would seem to risk the loss of much of the richness of feminist analysis of social and political power, and also to ignore some of the internal problems in the theoretical approaches mentioned thus far. Alternatively, we might choose to assert that in the light of the insights of postmodern argument, the only possible political response to the observed multiplicity of values, and the absence of any shared evaluative perspective that permits adjudication between them, is a political liberalism that permits the widest possible toleration of choices of life styles.[7] A slightly different route out of this impasse is provided by the methodological grounding of feminist theory exemplified in this volume.

The starting point of such an account is that, in the case of feminism, the tendency to tumble into skepticism about any statement of values is not a consequence of abstraction. Instead, and somewhat paradoxically, it arises because of feminism's very engagement with the social and political particularities of the lives of women. This engagement leads to a clear recognition of the differences between women, and of the complexity of the multiplicity of roles that women, and men, adopt at any one time and across their life cycles. However, this does not necessarily commit us to a relativistic paralysis. Rather, it leads us to two related strategies, both of which require us to acknowledge our role as participants in a political argument rather than as scientific observers of ethical reality.

Firstly, it would be argued, we need to recognize the validity of our own moral intuitions, and to provide a means of testing these against socially shared norms. The argument thus far suggests that we are complex subjects, ourselves historically and socially constituted with conflicting roles and multiple influences on our attitudes. But this does not necessarily empty us of the possession of values; rather, it might be argued that it requires that we recognize that our values are not universal and abstractly provable but that they arise out of a historical, social, and cultural experience of that which is good and that which is bad, and of that which we cannot tolerate.[8]

Secondly, it is claimed, we need to accept that the process of clarification of values is not one of abstract argument, but rather one of constant revision and debate about which versions of the values that we share make most sense of our moral and our empirical experiences. This fits closely with the methodology advocated by Walzer. He has suggested that the role of the social critic is that of a prophet,[9] who must seek to draw out the weakness and incoherences extant in the value system of the society in question, rather than to impose on it an external and unrelated system of ethics. Political theory, therefore, is a political and not a philosophical endeavor, and it is one that involves us in a continuing dialogue between competing versions of the possible ordering of the values. There may be no single "best reading" of our value system, but rather several competing political and ideological claims about the way in which our community ought to be organized. Our task as political participants, and as feminists, is to make our own political case persuasively about the way in which women will achieve the dignity and status to which we believe they are entitled, in terms that will make sense to those we address.

To apply this interpretation to the issue of a feminist reading or readings of international human rights would suggest two strategies. Firstly, it would require a strong declarative political statement of our own beliefs about the violations of women's dignity and status that we observe. This is found in different forms in all of the lectures in this volume. Secondly, it would require us to recognize the complexity and internal variability of our own culture and that of other societies. In order to make any specific case for the assertion of women's rights, we would be committed to examining the many roles and conditions of women's lives within a particular culture in order to a build a political argument which engages with that situation, and with the values and beliefs held by those women. This line of argument is taken up in the comments that Sarah Ansari and I make in response to Shere Hite's lecture, while specific analysis of particular impediments to the rights of women are explored by the individual lecturers.

To take this approach would, therefore, be to acknowledge that universal human rights, as a category, are problematic. But nevertheless, to declare them makes a vital point, and the rhetoric of rights serves important political functions that constitute a vibrant contribution to the international debate on ethical questions. At the same time, however, without abandoning our own evaluative commitments, it is necessary also to pursue a more sensitive approach to the exploration of the particular social sources of women's oppression, and to the appropriate response to them in the cultural circumstances of the case in hand. The reflective process by which feminist writers, in almost all traditions, derive and test their theoretical assumptions in the light of empirical data and sociological exploration, means that feminist political theory is well fitted to this task. Feminism, therefore, provides a critique that helps to explore the sources of oppression, for both women and men (as both French and le Doeuff specifically note). While not claiming that any of the authors would necessarily endorse this methodological perspective, it does seem that each lecture offers its own contribution to the process of the exploration of the values of Western societies, and the sources of the oppression of women within them, while many also provide a political contribution to the argument over the international context in which women's status seems to be under constant threat.

In the remainder of this introduction I will try to indicate the way in which the individual essays explore the issues of women's human rights in the authors' own voices. The first two pieces are works of liberal political theory. Martha Nussbaum provides a vigorous defense of liberalism as an essential vehicle for feminism. She points out that the language of liberalism, with its stress on personal autonomy and the value of the individual, provides a language in which women throughout the world can come to recognize and confront their oppression. Nussbaum argues that feminist attacks on liberalism are misplaced and seeks to demonstrate the methodological strength and the coherence, and indeed the central value for women, of the liberal commitment to individualism, abstraction, and reason. In particular, she resists Noddings's attempt to ground a "different" female form of ethics in the emotional, nonreasonable, "caring" response of the mother. Nussbaum does, nevertheless, accept that feminism can offer a valuable internal critique of liberalism, by indicating that liberalism, particularly in the "private sphere," has "failed to be individualistic enough." Thus liberal feminism enables one to hone the philosophy of liberalism and to choose between the competing variants of the philosophy. However, she insists, liberalism remains a "radical vision" that "should and can lead to social revolution," a vision that insists that all—men and women—should be "seen as human, rather than as someone's lord, or someone's subject." It is this vision, she argues, that will enable women to overturn the sources of their oppression.

In the second piece, Onora O'Neill also provides a powerful defense of liberalism. However, she does so by rejecting the reliance of many liberals, and others, on the language of rights. Rather, she insists, ethical theory should start with a concentration on our "obligations," so that to take rights, including women's rights, seriously is to take seriously the "obligations which are their counterparts."

To do otherwise has two pitfalls. Firstly, O'Neill argues that while all rights necessarily have concomitant obligations, not all obligations generate rights. To do otherwise than to "start" with a theory of obligations "is about as sensible as trying to count the adult population of a country by counting all the parents, so overlooking all childless persons." In particular, she argues that this can lead to a failure to discuss in liberal terms the "virtues" of care and concern that feminists and others have "properly insisted are ethically important." Hence, she denies the validity of the "difference" feminist case about a specifically feminine approach to ethics, which she suggests relies paradoxically on a faulty implicit theory of "real patriarchy" as providing a private domain in which the virtues of care can flourish. Instead, O'Neill substitutes what is in her view a stronger, liberal account of ethical virtue.

Secondly, she suggests, to concentrate on rights without specifying the relevant obligations can lead to laziness in terms of the identification of the institutional processes through which these rights are to be obtained. The result is a failure to ground rights in a clear account of the political and social mechanisms that will lead to their delivery, and of the ethical justification for these mechanisms. This, she argues, may lead to too weak a grounding of rights, such as welfare rights, which may have particular significance for women (though, she insists, such significance is contingent and is not the result of inherent female "difference"). If, instead, obligations are taken seriously, the result will be a powerful ethical claim for "allocations of obligations to deliver goods and services that take account of the realities of different sorts of lives."

The next three contributions turn to rather more sociological and anthropological accounts of why the language of "women's rights" is problematic. Marilyn French examines the way in which women have been presumed to be "less than fully human." One major source and support of this presumption is, she argues, religion, with each of the major religions of the world containing a strong presumption of male superiority. A second element is to be found in the assumptions of economic theory, and in the construction of economic systems worldwide. Here her feminist analysis runs in parallel with that of "green" political thought, with its emphasis on the inadequate measurement of economic goods. French suggests that this systematically undervalues the contribution of women, leading to policies that disempower women and also cause economic failure because of the misallocation of resources away from female producers to male consumers. The result of the low value accorded to women, and to their social and economic contribution, is widespread discrimination and violence against them.

French then documents the way in which women throughout the world, by recognizing and confronting their oppression, and by organizing, have attempted to redress the discrimination and abuse that they suffer. But more than this, she suggests, in their attempts to understand their own oppression women also gain confidence in their own ethical judgements, in those values disregarded by male policy makers. As a result, in many of the world's most terrible conflicts it has been women who have taken the initiative in finding a route to peace. Women have also played a central role in ecological movements.

However, French cautions against overoptimism. In particular, although women may achieve rights "on paper," these will have little value unless "male prejudice" is also confronted. Thus in the final section of her lecture, French gives an account of the construction of masculinity on the basis of repression and violence, which in itself gives rise to the pervasive oppression of women. She argues further that because of recent changes in the world economy, driven by the logic of the "masculine mystique," both men and women face a return to a political and economic system in which all live in fear. Only feminism offers an alternative to this miserable future.

Naomi Wolf too focuses on the issue of why "human rights" do not necessarily belong "naturally" to women. She presents a persuasive argument about the way in which "honor" and sexual dignity are crucial to women's equal enjoyment of rights. Sexual humiliation, she claims, is a means by which women learn to understand themselves as less than fully human. In this respect, sexually denigrating banter and dirty jokes are part of a spectrum that runs to the routine sexual degradation of female political prisoners. Far from being innocuous, on the one hand, or contingent to the terrorization of the general population, on the other, this denial of sexual dignity does crucial "work" in the stripping away of the "honor" and personal dignity that are a necessary part of individual integrity. Women are thereby inculcated with the message that they are "less than" men, that they are indeed second-class citizens. This "anthropological" mechanism runs alongside systems of formal equality, removing their substance and legitimating the continuing discrimination against women. For Wolf, therefore, liberalism and rights theory will always fail if they restrict themselves to the codification of values instead of engaging with the social sources and supports of male power.

Michèle le Doeuff, in her lecture "Each Man in His Cave," also addresses the relations of authority and social practice that determine male power. She examines the institution of matrimony and suggests, in a multilayered and subtle argument, that male power over women, far from being "natural," is an instance of the power and interests of the state. Marriage is only attractive to men, she argues, where it permits male domination over women, but it is the institution of marriage itself, through the legal forms determined by states, that constructs male sexuality as predatory and violent.

Thus the structures and practices that constitute marriage, although rarely the subject of political discourse or debate, constitute an intensively political institution. The source of states' interest in the forms of marriage is their concern with what she describes as a "pronatalist" policy. Consequently, where women gain control of reproduction and fertility, the significance of marriage for the state declines. This implies that feminism succeeds, in part, because of new contraceptive technologies, but also that the right to control their fertility is a crucial one for women. More generally, the private sphere is the central realm and source of male power and of the state's entrenchment of women's powerlessness. Any attempt to enshrine rights for women must, therefore, reinforce the tentative moves towards the recognition of the relevance of the private sphere for women's rights made in recent international human rights law.

The final lecture in this volume is by Shere Hite. It contains a powerful polemic about the current position of women in the face of what she views as their loss of ground following the reassertion of "fundamentalist" religious beliefs throughout the world. She attributes this resurgence of religious commitment to the failure of liberalism to make clear its own value system, and its weakness in response to authoritarian challenges. Women are the main losers in this set of changes, although men too are increasingly subject to intolerant legal systems. Feminism, she argues, contains the ethical content and political will to challenge the "new politics," so that the success of feminist politics, and the achievement of women's human rights, is vital for all of us, men and women.

Hite's lecture was originally presented in a questioning and challenging style which called out for audience response. Because of this, and because of the way in which it raises issues that are difficult and challenging for feminism and which are also touched on by many of the other lectures, the printed version of Hite's lecture has been interwoven with a set of responses. These seek to reflect on and expand the themes raised by Hite, and others, particularly with respect to the way in which feminists and rights theorists respond to different cultures (especially Islamic culture), while also drawing together the central themes of the lecture series.

The conclusion that we might draw from these lectures is that to focus on the category of gender is to focus on a sphere of failure and incoherence in the field of human rights. As such, it as an excellent source of reflection on the substance and significance of claims of rights, and of the factors that stand in the way of their equal enjoyment. This is particularly so since, as many of these pieces show, one is quickly drawn from a focus on women into the wider contexts of cultural identity, race, and religion.

Introduction 11

To speak from the perspective of women, to adopt a woman's voice, is therefore to enrich our understanding of the "rights" of all.

Notes

1. *In a Different Voice: Psychological Theory and Women's Development* (Cambridge: Harvard University Press, 1992). This piece has been widely discussed and was incorporated into an argument between "equality" and "difference" feminists as discussed in Gisella Bock and Susan James, *Beyond Equality and Difference: Citizenship, Feminist Politics, and Female Subjectivity* (London: Routledge, 1992), esp. the introduction, pp. 1–17.

2. The primary texts here are Nel Noddings, *Caring: A Feminine Approach to Ethics and Moral Education* (Berkeley: University of California Press, 1984); and Sara Ruddick, *Maternal Thinking: Towards a Politics of Peace* (London: Women's Press, 1990).

3. For intelligent and critical discussions of these categories, see Rosemarie Tong, *Feminist Thought: A Comprehensive Introduction* (Boulder, Colo.: Westview, 1989); or Valerie Bryson, *Feminist Political Theory: An Introduction* (Basingstoke, U.K.: Macmillan, 1992).

4. For example, Susan Moller Okin, *Justice, Gender, and the Family* (New York: Basic Books, 1989).

5. See, for example, bell hooks, *Ain't I a Woman: Black Women and Feminism* (Boston: South End, 1981).

6. One might note the example of genital mutilation (clitoridectomy or genital infibulation) which is referred to by several of the authors.

7. This is the argument developed in Richard Rorty, *Contingency, Irony, and Solidarity* (Cambridge: Cambridge University Press, 1989). See also the critical discussion by Stephen Mulhall and Adam Swift, *Liberals and Communitarians* (Oxford: Blackwell, 1992), pp. 232–248.

8. This is one of the implications of the argument developed by Charles Taylor in "Atomism," in *Philosophy and the Human Understanding: Philosophical Papers 2* (Cambridge: Cambridge University Press, 1985), pp. 187–210, esp. pp. 204–207.

9. See Michael Walzer, "The Prophet as Social Critic," in *Interpretation and Social Criticism* (Cambridge: Harvard University Press, 1987), pp. 67–95.

1

The Feminist Critique of Liberalism

Martha Nussbaum

Women around the world are using the language of liberalism. Consider some representative examples from recent publications:

- Roop Rekha Verma, philosopher and grassroots activist from Lucknow, India, speaks about the many ways in which Indian religious traditions have devalued women. She concludes that the largest problem with these traditions is that they deprive women of "full personhood." "What is personhood?" Verma asks. "To me three things seem essential for [full personhood]: autonomy, self-respect, and a sense of fulfillment and achievement."[1]
- Nahid Toubia, the first woman surgeon in the Sudan and a woman's health activist, writes of the urgent need to mobilize international opposition to the practice of female genital mutilation, especially when it is performed on young girls without their consent. "International human rights bodies and organizations," she concludes, "must declare FGM to be violence against women and children and a violation of their rights.... If women are to be considered as equal and responsible members of society, no aspect of their physical, psychological, or sexual integrity can be compromised."[2]
- *The Hindu* magazine, describing a meeting at the Indian Institute of Management in Bangalore that brought together widows from all over India for a discussion of their living conditions, reports as follows:

> Throughout the week they came to realise many things about themselves and their lives—especially how much they had internalised society's perceptions of them as daughters, wives, mothers and widows (their identity invariably defined in terms of their relationship to men). . . . They were encouraged to see themselves as persons who had a right to exist even if their husbands were dead, and as citizens who had a right to resources—such as land, housing, employment, credit and ration cards—which would enable them to live and bring up their children (if any) with dignity and self-respect.[3]

Personhood, autonomy, rights, dignity, self-respect: These are the terms of the liberal Enlightenment. Women are using them, and teaching other women to use them when they did not use them before. They treat these terms as though they matter, as though they are the best terms in which to conduct a radical critique of society, as though using them is crucial to women's quality of life.

This situation looks in some respects deeply paradoxical, since liberalism has been thought by many feminists to be a political approach that is totally inadequate to the needs and aims of women, and in some ways profoundly subversive of those aims. Over the past twenty years feminist political thinkers have put forward many reasons to reject liberalism and to define feminism to some extent in opposition to liberalism. In 1983, in one of the most influential works of feminist political theory, Alison Jaggar concluded that "the liberal conception of human nature and of political philosophy cannot constitute the philosophical foundation for an adequate theory of women's liberation."[4] Many influential feminist thinkers have tended to agree with Jaggar, and to treat liberalism as at best negligent of women's concerns and at worst an active enemy of women's progress.

But liberalism has not died in feminist politics; if anything, with the dramatic growth of the movement to recognize various women's rights as central human rights under international law, its radical feminist potential is just beginning to be realized. So it is time to reassess the charges most commonly made in the feminist critique of liberalism to see whether they really give us good reasons to view the continued ascendancy of feminist liberalism with skepticism.

Who is this "us," and why should "our" conclusions matter? It is obvious that the activists from whom I have quoted have gone about their business undaunted by the feminist critique, and they will not be daunted now, if feminists once again tell them that autonomy and personhood are bad notions for feminists to use. In that sense a philosophical reassessment could be seen as beside the point. But the international political situation is volatile, and the liberal discourse of personhood and rights has come under attack from many directions, some of them practical and influential.[5] Looking at the case for the defense is therefore not simply a scholarly exercise, but also a contribution to practical politics.

I shall examine the feminist critique under three headings: (1) individualism and community, (2) abstraction and concrete reality, and (3) reason and emotion. In general, I shall argue, liberalism of a kind can be defended against the charges that have been made. The deepest and most central ideas of the liberal tradition are ideas of radical force and great theoretical and practical value. These ideas can be formulated in ways that incorporate what is most valuable in the feminist critique, although liberalism needs to learn from feminism if it is to formulate its own central insights in a fully adequate manner. Taking on board the insights of feminism will not leave liberalism unchanged, and liberalism needs to change to respond adequately to those insights. But it will be changed in ways that make it more deeply consistent with its own most foundational ideas. Another way of expressing this point is to say that there have been many varieties of liberalism and many strands within liberalism; thinking about the feminist critique proves important in choosing among these varieties because feminism does show real weaknesses in some forms of liberalism that continue to be influential, though not, I shall argue, in the most basic ideas of liberalism itself. Some feminist proposals do resist incorporation even into a reformulated feminist liberalism; but I shall argue that these are proposals that should be resisted as we attempt to promote justice for the world's women.

There is danger in speaking so generally about "liberalism," a danger that has often plagued feminist debates. "Liberalism" is not a single position, but a family of positions; it is obvious that Kantian liberalism is profoundly different from classical utilitarian liberalism, and both of these from the utilitarianism currently dominant in neoclassical economics. Many critiques of liberalism are really critiques of economic utilitarianism, and would not hold against the views of Kant, or Mill. Some feminist attacks oversimplify the tradition, and in responding to them I run a grave risk of oversimplification myself. When I speak of "liberalism," then, I shall have in mind, above all, the tradition of Kantian liberalism represented today in the political thought of John Rawls, and also the classical utilitarian liberal tradition, especially as exemplified in the work of John Stuart Mill. I shall also refer frequently to some major precursors, namely, Jean-Jacques Rousseau, David Hume, and Adam Smith, who made enormously important contributions to the development of liberal ideas of equality and choice. It seems reasonable to assess the feminist critique by holding it up against the best examples of liberal political thought; any critique of liberalism that cannot be taken seriously as a criticism of Kant or Mill probably is not worth discussing.

The thinkers I have chosen are not in agreement on many important matters; but there is a core of common commitments that can be scrutinized with the interests of feminism in mind. At the heart of this tradition is a twofold intuition about human beings: namely, that all, just by being human, are of equal dignity and worth, no matter where they are situated in society; and that the primary source of this worth is a power of moral choice within them, a power that consists in the ability to plan a life in accordance with one's own evaluations of ends.[6] To these two intuitions—which link liberalism at its core to the thought of the Greek and Roman Stoics[7]—the liberal tradition adds one more, which the Stoics did not emphasize: The moral equality of persons gives them a fair claim to certain types of treatment at the hands of society and politics. What this treatment is will be a subject of debate within the tradition, but the shared starting point is that this treatment must do two closely related things. It must respect and promote the liberty of choice, and it must respect and promote the equal worth of persons as choosers.[8]

To what is liberalism, so conceived, opposed? Here again we must begin crudely, with some rough intuitions that we will try to render more precise as we go on. Liberalism is opposed, first of all, to any approach to politics that turns morally irrelevant differences into systematic sources of social hierarchy.[9] It is opposed, then, to the naturalizing of hierarchies—to the caste system characteristic of traditional Indian society; to related caste hierarchies created in many times and places by differences of race and class and power and religion.[10] It is opposed, second, to forms of political organization that are corporatist or organically organized—that seek a good for the group as a whole without focusing above all on the well-being and agency of individual group members.[11] Finally, it is opposed to a politics that is ideologically based, in the sense that it turns one particular conception of value—whether utopian or religious or traditional—into a mandatory standard imposed by authority on all citizens. Religious intolerance, the establishment of a single church, or the establishment of a single utopian political vision of the good—all of these strike the liberal as embodying unequal respect for persons, who ought to be free to follow their conscience in the most important matters. Liberalism is thus opposed to Marxism, to theocratic social orders, and to many forms of authoritarian or tradition-based conservatism.[12]

Liberalism so conceived is centrally about the protection of spheres of choice—not, I claim, in a purely negative way, maximizing the sheer number of choices people get to make for themselves, but rather in a way closely tied to the norm of equal respect for personhood. The choices that get protection will be those deemed to be of crucial importance to the protection and expression of personhood. Thus it would be perfectly consistent for a liberal, beginning from these intuitions, to support certain forms of interference with choice if it could be successfully argued that such interference promotes equal respect rather than undermining it, or, even, that the interference makes no difference to personhood one way or another. All liberal views accept some interference with choice, whether to promote more choice, or to constrain force and fraud, or to produce greater overall prosperity, or greater fairness. Starting from the same basic intuitions, then, liberals can end up in very different positions about many matters, such as the justice of various types of economic redistribution, or the appropriateness of various types of paternalistic legislation. They will differ about these policies because they differ about what is crucial in order to respect the equal worth of persons and to give the power of choice the support that is its due. On this account, both John Rawls and Robert Nozick are liberals because both share a central commitment to liberty and equal respect, although they disagree profoundly about the permissibility of economic redistribution—Rawls holding that it is required in order to show equal respect for persons and Nozick holding that it is incompatible with such equal respect.[13] Many such disagreements arise within liberalism. They involve, often, not only disagreement about means to shared ends, but also different concrete specifications of some highly general ends.[14] On the other hand, it would be hard to conceive of a form of liberalism in which religious toleration was not a central tenet, or one that did not protect certain basic freedoms associated with personal choice, such as freedoms of expression, press, and assembly.[15]

Feminists have made three salient charges against this liberal tradition as a philosophy that might be used to promote women's goals. They have charged, first, that it is too "individualistic": that its focus on the dignity and worth of the individual slights and unfairly subordinates the value to be attached to community and to collective social entities such as families, groups, and classes. They have charged, second, that its ideal of equality is too abstract and formal, that it errs through lack of immersion in the concrete realities of power in different social situations. Finally, they have charged that liberalism errs through its focus on reason, unfairly slighting the role we should give to emotion and care in the moral and political life. All these alleged failings in liberalism are linked to specific failings in the tradition's handling of women's issues. It has frequently been claimed that liberalism cannot atone for these defects without changing utterly and that feminists interested in progress beyond the status quo would be better off choosing a different political philosophy—whether a form of socialism or Marxism, or a form of communitarian or care-based political theory. Let us examine these charges.

Individual and Community

The most common feminist charge against liberalism is that it is too "individualistic." By taking the individual to be the basic unit for political thought, it treats the individual as prior to society, as capable (in theory if not in fact) of existing outside of all social ties. "Logically if not empirically," writes Jaggar of the liberal view, "human individuals could exist outside a social context; their essential characteristics, their needs and interests, their capacities and desires, are given independently of their social context and are not created or even fundamentally altered by that context."[16] Jaggar later restates this liberal "metaphysical assumption" in an even stronger form: "Each human individual has desires, interests, etc. that in principle can be fulfilled quite separately from the desires and interests of other people."[17] Jaggar later describes this as the liberal assumption of "political solipsism, the assumption that human individuals are essentially self-sufficient entities."[18] She holds that this starting point makes liberals characterize "community and cooperation . . . as phenomena whose existence and even possibility is puzzling," if not downright "impossible."[19]

Described this way, liberal individualism lies perilously close to two positions most feminists agree in rejecting: *egoism* and *normative self-sufficiency*. If liberals really did hold, as Jaggar suggests, that the most basic desires of human beings are not only not shaped by society but also are desires that can be satisfied independently of the satisfactions of desires and interests of others, they would indeed be close to endorsing *psychological egoism*, the view that people are all motivated to pursue their own self-interest above all else. And this, of course, is a view that makes cooperation and community at least somewhat puzzling. On the basis of Jaggar's belief that such self-centered desires and interests are given special weight in liberal politics, she apparently takes the liberal view to lie close to *normative ethical egoism* as well,[20] that is, to a view that it is always best to promote the satisfaction of one's own self-interest—though such a conclusion is rather puzzling given that the political theories she discusses, both Utilitarian and Rawlsian, aim, by Jaggar's own account, at satisfying *everyone's* interests, not just the interests of a single agent. This would seem to make them far from egoistic.[21]

The charge of egoism is unconvincing. Some liberal thinkers do assume a form of psychological egoism, and it is right of both feminists and others to call that assumption into question. Jaggar cites Amartya Sen's article "Rational Fools,"[22] which criticizes economic utilitarianism for underrating the importance of sympathy and commitment as motives; she is right to find this a powerful objection to some dominant modes of economic modeling. But she herself admits that this view of human motivation is far from universal in the liberal tradition: that John Rawls has a nonegoistic account of human psychology, and that Mill and Kant think of the human being as conflicted by egoistic and nonegoistic motives.[23] She does not give us any reason to believe that the egoism she criticizes in economic utilitarianism is entailed or even encouraged by anything deep in liberalism itself.

Indeed, even Jaggar's weaker psychological claim about the solitary character of basic desires in liberalism appears to be inaccurate. Liberal theorists vary, and no doubt some, in particular Hobbes[24] and Bentham in their different ways, come close to imagining the human individual as having no natural love of others. Kant, because he holds that all sensuous inclinations are accidents of individual endowment, is agnostic on the matter, and thinks that we should not rely on such motives too much if we want to promote benevolence. But other liberal thinkers, such as Rousseau, Mill, Hume, Smith, and Rawls, have an evidently social and other-inclusive psychology, building in affiliation with and need for others into the very foundations of their accounts of human motivation, and denying that individuals can satisfy their basic desires independently of relationship and community. In a very important way Kant himself agrees: for although he holds that with respect to liking and pleasure and other forms of sensuous inclination we are not reliably inclined toward one another, he holds at the same time that the identity of a human being is given in the most fundamental terms by its membership in a certain sort of community, namely, the kingdom of ends, the community of free, rational beings who regard one another with respect and awe and who are committed to promote one another's happiness and well-being because of the respect they feel for one another. Rawls, similarly, imagines the agents in the Original Position as held together by a concern for building a community in which they will live together on terms of mutual cooperation.

As for normative ethical egoism, one could not even begin to argue plausibly that either the utilitarian or the Kantian tradition is guilty. The essential emphasis of liberal individualism is on respect for *others* as individuals; how can this even initially be thought to involve egoism? Both theories are extremely exigent in the demands they make of moral agents in respect of altruism and duties to others. Utilitarianism holds that an action is right only if it maximizes total or average utility—of all the world's people, in its strictest version; some utilitarians would extend the requirement to animals as well. Clearly this is a theory that demands enormous sacrifices of agents, and it is very far from letting them go about their self-interested business. Kantian duties to others are not quite as severe, since "imperfect duties" of benevolence have much elasticity, and the Kantian agent is allowed to give preference on many occasions to the near and dear. Nonetheless, it would be utterly implausible to call Kant's an egoistic moral theory, since duties to promote the happiness of others are at its very core.[25]

More initially plausible is the suggestion that liberalism, by conceiving the human being in a way that imagines her cut off from all others and yet thriving, encourages normative projects of self-sufficiency—urges people, that is, to minimize their needs for one another and to depend on themselves alone. This, I think, is what Jaggar is really worried about when she speaks of "political solipsism." This is certainly one of the charges feminists commonly think true of liberalism, and one of the ways in which feminists have connected liberalism with common male attitudes and concerns. Feminists hold that by encouraging self-sufficiency as a goal, liberalism subverts the values of family and community, ends that feminists rightly prize. What should we say about this charge?

First, we should note that the normative goal of self-sufficiency is not one that feminists should dismiss without an argument. Those figures in the Western philosophical tradition who have defended some form of detachment and self-sufficiency as human goals—in particular, the Stoics and Spinoza—have done so using powerful arguments, in particular arguments that connect the aim of self-sufficiency with the elimination of anger and revenge, and the creation of a just and merciful society. Even should feminists wish ultimately to reject those arguments, they need to grapple with them, rather than viewing them as so many signs of heedless maleness.[26]

Second, we should observe that the ethical aim of self-sufficiency and detachment is not strongly linked to individualism, that is, to the view that the primary focus of ethical and political thought should be the individual, understood as a separate unit. Indeed, in its most influential world form, in the Buddhist and to some extent also Hindu traditions, the normative doctrine of self-sufficiency and detachment presupposes the recognition that individuals as such do not really exist; it is precisely this recognition that grounds indifference to events, such as deaths of loved ones, that might be thought to matter deeply. Individualism, with its focus on what happens here and now in one's very own life, would seem to have an uphill battle in order to cultivate detachment from such external events.[27]

Next, we should remark that even were the psychology of liberalism as described, that is, even if liberals did hold that our most basic desires can be satisfied independently of relationships to others, the normative conclusions about self-sufficiency would not follow. For moral theories frequently demand of people things that go against the grain, and we could demand great concern for others from people to whom such concern does not seem to come naturally. Such appears to have been the enterprise of Jeremy Bentham, who combined an extremely self-centered psychology with an exigent normative altruism. Kant, too, was ready to demand of agents that they disregard their most powerful desires; he famously holds that even a man in whose heart nature has placed little sympathy for others can still be expected to be absolutely committed to their good, both in family and in community. Kant certainly believes that all altruistic commitment and loving concern in marriage goes against the grain, given the extremely solipsistic tendencies he imputes to sexual desire; but he expected individuals to live up to those commitments rather than seek self-sufficiency.[28] Liberals, then, can and do highly value benevolence, family concern, and social/political involvement, even if they should hold that individuals need to control strong selfish inclinations and have little inclination or liking for these things. And, as I have argued, liberalism typically endows individuals with powerful other-regarding motives also.

Liberal individualism, then, does not entail either egoism or normative self-sufficiency. What does it really mean, then, to make the individual the basic unit for political thought? It means, first of all, that liberalism responds sharply to the basic fact that each person has a course from birth to death that is not precisely the same as that of any other person; that each person is one and not more than one; that each feels pain in his or her own body; that the food given to A does not arrive in the stomach of B. The separateness of persons is a basic fact of human life; in stressing it, liberalism stresses something experientially true, and fundamentally important. In stressing this fact, the liberal takes her stand squarely in the camp of this-worldly experience and rejects forms of revisionary metaphysics (for example, forms of Buddhism or of Platonism) that would deny the reality of our separateness and our substantial embodied character.[29] It rejects the Buddhist picture of persons as mere whorls in the ceaseless flux of world energy and the feudal picture of persons as fundamentally characterized by a set of hierarchical relations. It says that the fundamental entity for politics is a living body that goes from here to there, from birth to death, never fused with any other—that we are hungry and joyful and loving and needy one by one, however closely we may embrace one another.[30] In normative terms, this commitment to the recognition of individual separateness means, for the liberal, that the demands of a collectivity or a relation should not, as such, be made the basic goal of politics. Collectivities, such as the state and even the family, are composed of individuals, who never do fuse, who always continue to have their separate brains and voices and stomachs, however much they love one another. Each one of these is separate, and each one of these is an end. Liberalism holds that the flourishing of human beings taken one by one is both analytically and normatively prior to the flourishing of the state or the nation or the religious group: analytically, because such unities do not really efface the separate reality of individual lives and normatively, because the recognition of that separateness is held to be a fundamental fact for ethics, which should recognize each separate entity as an end, not as a means to the ends of others. The central question of politics should be not, How is the organic whole doing? but How are X and Y and Z and Q doing? Then the central goal for politics will be some sort of amelioration in the lives of X and Y and Z and Q, where a larger amount of happiness for X, where X might be the ruler, does not compensate for a larger amount of misery for Q, where Q might be a poor rural woman.[31]

Putting things this way does not require us to deny that X might love Y intensely, and view his life as worthless without Y; it does not require that Z and Q do not plan their lives together and aim at shared ends; it does not require us to hold that all four do not need one another profoundly, or vividly hold the pleasure and pain of one another in their imaginations. It just asks us to concern ourselves with the distribution of resources and opportunities in a certain way, namely, with concern to see how well *each and every one of them* is doing, seeing each and every one as an end, worthy of concern.

Put this way, liberal individualism seems to be a very good view for feminists to embrace. For it is clear that women have too rarely been treated as ends in themselves, and all too frequently treated as means to the ends of others. Women's individual well-being has far too rarely been taken into account in political and economic planning and measurement. Women have very often been treated as parts of a larger unit, especially the family, and valued primarily for their contribution as reproducers and caregivers, rather than as sources of agency and worth in their own right. In connection with this nonindividualistic way of valuing women, questions about families have been asked without asking how well each of its individual members are doing. But conflicts for resources and opportunities are ubiquitous in families around the world, and women are often the victims of these conflicts. When food is scarce in families, it is very frequently women, and especially girls, who get less, who become malnourished and die. When there is an illness and only some children can be taken to the doctor, it is frequently girls who are neglected. Amartya Sen's well-known statistic of "missing women" estimates that 100 million women are not alive in the world today who would have been alive had they received nutrition and health care equal to that given to males. There are 44 million such "missing women" in China alone, 36.9 million in India. In India the "missing women" comprise 9.5 percent of the number of actual women, in Pakistan, 12.9 percent. Again, when only some children can go to school, it is frequently the girls who are kept at home. In South Asia, female literacy rates average around half those of males. In some countries the ratio is still lower; for example, in Afghanistan, 32 percent, in Sudan, 27 percent.[32]

Again, when there is violence in the family, women and girls are overwhelmingly likely to be its victims. Here there are depressingly many statistics, but to cite just a few: The UN *Human Development Report* for

1995 reports that one-third of women in Barbados, Canada, the Netherlands, New Zealand, Norway, and the United States report sexual abuse during childhood or adolescence. Each year, an estimated one million children (mostly girls in Asia) are forced into prostitution, often with the connivance of their families. There are estimated 85–100 million women alive today who have suffered genital mutilation.[33] In Colombia during 1982 and 1983, the Forensic Institute of Bogotá found that of 1,170 cases of bodily injury, one of five was due to conjugal violence, and 94 percent of those hospitalized were battered women. More than 50 percent of married women in the largest slum of Bangkok reported being regularly beaten by their husbands.[34] In the maternity hospital of Lima, Peru, 90 percent of all young mothers aged twelve to sixteen have been raped by their father, stepfather, or another close relative. In Costa Rica, an agency working with young mothers reports that 95 percent of their pregnant clients under age fifteen are victims of incest. U.S. data show that 29 percent of female rape victims are age ten and under, 62 percent are age fifteen and under.[35] As for marriage itself, many of the world's women do not have the right to consent to a marriage, and few have any recourse from ill-treatment within it. Divorce, even if legally available, is commonly not a practical option, given women's economic dependency and lack of educational and employment opportunities. Marital rape is a ubiquitous fact of female life; both Western and non-Western nations have been culpably slow to criminalize it.[36]

To people who live in the midst of such facts, it is very important to say, "I am a separate person and an individual. I count for something as such, and my pain is not wiped out by someone else's satisfaction." When we reflect that a large number of the world's women inhabit traditions that really have denied the separateness of persons, and that many more inhabit traditions that, whatever their metaphysics, value women primarily for the care they give to others rather than as ends, we have all the more reason to insist that liberal individualism is good for women.[37]

There is no doubt that liberalism deserves feminist criticism on this point. For, as many feminists have long pointed out, where women and the family are concerned, liberal political thought has not been nearly individualist enough. Liberal thinkers tended to segment the private from the public sphere, considering the public sphere to be the sphere of individual rights and contractual arrangements, the family to be a private sphere of love and comfort into which the state should not meddle. This tendency grows, no doubt, out of a legitimate concern for the protection of choice—but too few questions have been asked about whose choices are thereby protected. Liberals have often failed to notice the extent to which law and institutional arrangements shape the family institution and determine the privileges and rights of its members. Having failed to notice this, they all too frequently have failed to ask whether there are legal deficiencies in this sphere that urgently need addressing. In 1869 John Stuart Mill already urged British law to address the problem of marital rape, which, he said, made the lot of women lower than that of slaves:

> Hardly any slave . . . is a slave at all hours and all minutes. . . . But it cannot be so with the wife. Above all, a female slave has (in Christian countries) an admitted right, and is considered under a moral obligation, to refuse to her master the last familiarity. Not so the wife: however brutal a tyrant she may unfortunately be chained to—though she may know that he hates her, though it may be his daily pleasure to torture her, and though she may feel it impossible not to loathe him—he can claim from her and enforce the lowest degradation of a human being, that of being made the instrument of an animal function contrary to her inclinations.[38]

Though Mill seems excessively sanguine here about the female slave,[39] he is right on target about the wife, and he sees what a deep violation of basic liberal tenets is involved in the failure to legislate against marital rape. Again, in the same passage, he argues that the laws that deny the wife equal legal rights over children are also a profound violation of personhood and autonomy.[40] In a similar way, he diagnoses other distortions of the family structure caused by male power and the laws that expressed it, arguing for women's full equality in all that relates to citizenship, and therefore for many changes in disabling family laws.

Mill supports his argument in part by appeal to consistency, saying that liberalism cannot plausibly deny women the rights it vindicates for men. But he also argues that *male* citizenship in a liberal regime is ill served by a mode of family organization based upon subordination. For such a family order is a vestige of monarchical power, and raises up little despots who are ill prepared to respect the rights and dignity of their fellow citizens.

> Think what it is to a boy, to grow up to manhood in the belief that without any merit or any exertion of his own, though he may be the most frivolous and empty or the most ignorant and stolid of mankind, by the mere fact of being born a male he is by right the superior of all and every one of an entire half of the human race: including probably some whose real superiority to himself he has daily or hourly occasion to feel. . . . Is it imagined that all this does not pervert the whole manner of existence of the man, both as an individual and as a social being? It is an exact parallel to the feeling of a hereditary king that he is excellent above others by being born a king, or a noble by being born a noble. The relation between husband and wife is very like that between lord and vassal, except that the wife is held to more unlimited obedience than the vassal was. However the vassal's character may have been

> affected, for better or worse, by his subordination, who can help seeing that the lord's was affected greatly for the worse? ... The self-worship of the monarch, or of the feudal superior, is matched by the self-worship of the male. Human beings do not grow up from childhood in the possession of unearned distinctions, without pluming themselves upon them.[41]

In short, Mill argues, the stability of a liberal regime demands the legal reform of family structure. All liberals should and must seek the "advantage of having the most universal and pervading of all human relations regulated by justice instead of injustice."[42]

Mill's arguments in *The Subjection of Women* showed that a concern for the individual well-being of family members, and a determination to use law and public policy to further that concern, were in no way alien to liberalism. Indeed, they grew naturally, as he shows, out of liberalism's concern for the fair treatment of each and every individual and its disdain for feudalism and monarchical power, for the castelike ascendancy of morally irrelevant distinctions. But most of the liberal tradition did not follow Mill's lead. Thus John Rawls, while envisaging a society in which each individual's well-being would be a matter of social concern, still imagined the contracting individuals as heads of households who would be expected to take thought altruistically for the interests of family members.[43] Here Rawls adopted a strategy similar to that of economist Gary Becker, whose model of the family has had enormous influence on information gathering and policy modeling around the world. Becker held that for purposes of modeling we should assume that the head of the household is a beneficent altruist who will adequately take thought for the interests of all family members.[44] Liberal reluctance to interfere with the family has run very deep, and shockingly many liberal thinkers have not noticed that the family is not in fact always characterized by a harmony of interest, that males are not always beneficent altruists.[45] No model of the family can be adequate to reality if it fails to take account of competition for scarce resources, divergent interests, and differences of power.[46]

Liberalism has much to learn from feminism in this area. It should begin by learning the facts of women's hunger, domestic violence, marital rape, and unequal access to education. It should go on to correct these facts by laws and by moral education. It should also consider the implications of women's individuality for many traditional areas of law and policy, prominently including divorce and taxation.[47] But notice that, as Mill already argued, what we see here is not a failure intrinsic to liberalism itself. It is, in fact, a failure of liberal thinkers to follow their own thought through to its socially radical conclusion. What is wrong with the views of the family endorsed by Becker, Rawls, and others is not that they are too individualist, but that they are not individualist enough. They assume too much organic unity and harmony. They give people too much credit for altruism and are not worried enough about the damages of competition. For this reason they fail to ask rigorously their own question, namely, how is each and every individual doing? They fail to ask this, perhaps, because they are focused on the autonomy and freedom of males, and they want to give these males plenty of scope for planning their lives in the private sphere. But that is not the liberal tradition, when this freedom is bought at the expense of violence and death to other individuals. To treat males this way is, as Mill said, tantamount to treating them as kings, who have a hereditary title to subordinate others. To treat any group or person this way runs counter to the deepest instincts of the liberal tradition. Despotism must be curtailed by laws protecting the equality of citizens, whether or not this despotism occurs within the family. The public conception of a liberal society should be a place of refuge and dignity for those whose personal relations, without legal intervention, would not have guaranteed this dignity.

Notice that Mill claims not only that these reforms are just and that they protect the dignity and well-being of women. He claims, as well, that they are essential to promoting the dignity and well-being of men. Hierarchy is bad for the ruler too. Instead of proper self-respect, he develops vanity; instead of relations of reciprocity and mutuality, he becomes habituated to relationships of exploitation and use. "In this sense," comments Roop Rekha Verma, developing these points in the context of contemporary India, "the feminist struggle must be viewed as the struggle for the liberation of humanity as a whole."[48] But that struggle, against the background of feudalism, is what liberalism is all about.

For these reasons major theoretical and practical attempts to remedy the wrongs done to women in the family have been able to propose internal criticisms of liberalism, rather than its wholesale rejection. Susan Moller Okin's *Justice, Gender, and the Family* criticizes liberal theory severely for its failure to consider injustice in the family. But she argues, plausibly, that John Rawls's theory of justice can be reformulated—along lines suggested by Rawls himself when he insisted that the family was one of the institutions that are part of the "basic structure of society" to be ordered in accordance with principles of justice.[49] In this feminist reformulation, parties in the original position would be individuals rather than representatives of household units;[50] and parties in the original position, in addition to being ignorant of their wealth, class, and conception of the good, would also be ignorant of their sex. Okin argues that this would lead them to design institutions in which the influence of gender (that is, of the social hierarchies correlated with biological sex) was minimized, and opportunities and resources would be equitably distributed within the family.[51] Rawls appears to have accepted this proposal.[52]

In a very similar manner, international women's activists, taking international human rights agencies to task for their neglect of issues such as marital rape, domestic violence, marital consent, and women's hunger, have not moved to jettison the language of human rights. Instead, they have insisted that the major rights already on the agenda be vindicated for women, and also that rights of women to be free from gender-specific abuses be added to the list of human rights. Once again, the defect found in international agencies such as the United Nations is not that they have stressed individualism too much, but that, deferring to tradition and male power, they have not done so consistently and deeply enough. Charlotte Bunch, who coordinated the Global Campaign for Women's Human Rights at the United Nations 1993 World Conference on Human Rights, eloquently describes the feminist liberal program:

> The concept of human rights, like all vibrant visions, is not static or the property of any one group; rather, its meaning expands as people reconceive of their needs and hopes in relation to it. In this spirit, feminists redefine human rights abuses to include the degradation and violation of women.[53]

This liberal program is already producing transformations in many countries. Some rights language in constitutions and statutes around the world is vague and aspirational, of little help to women who actually suffer from abuse. But there is indeed change. Consider a 1982 case in Bangladesh, *Nelly Zaman v. Ghiyasuddin*.[54] A woman trapped in a violent and abusive marriage sought to exercise her legal right to divorce. The husband challenged, seeking restitution of his conjugal rights. Although the woman's right to divorce was clearly established by the marriage contract, the lower court held that she had "no right to divorce at her own sweet will and without any reasonable excuse." Her rights were vindicated by the High Court, which commented as follows:

> The very concept of the husband's unilateral plea for forcible restitution of conjugal rights had become outmoded and ... does not fit with the State and Public Principle and Policy of equality of all men and women being citizens equal before the law and entitled to be treated only in accordance with the law as guaranteed in Articles 27 and 31 of the Constitution.[55]

In such small victories, which, taken cumulatively, can have a radical impact on the conduct of daily life,[56] women have been winning the right to be recognized as separate beings, beings whose well being is distinct from that of a husband's, and who have a life of their own to live. In a similar manner, the widows who gathered in Bangalore were learning to think of themselves not as discarded adjuncts of a family unit, half-dead things, but as centers of thought and choice and action, citizens who could make claims against the state for respect and for resources. All this is liberal individualism; and liberal individualism, consistently followed through, entails a radical feminist program. Most liberal political thinkers of the past have not consistently followed out this program. While talking about separateness and personhood, they did not take the separate personhood of women seriously enough. While objecting to some instances of feudal and monarchical power, they did not object to that power when it was justified by the accident of gender. Whether this omission is explained by convention or cowardice or disdain or inadvertence, it is culpable, and it has done great harm. But we see here the failure of people, not the failure of liberalism.

A deep strategic question arises at this point. When liberal people and states prove obtuse, refusing women's legitimate demands to be treated as ends, at what point should women—in pursuit of that liberal end—prefer revolutionary strategies that depart from liberal politics? Many feminists have discovered that Mill is correct: "the generality of the male sex cannot yet tolerate the idea of living with an equal." In consequence, legitimate arguments are met, again and again, not with rational engagement but with a resistance that keeps "throwing up fresh entrenchments of argument to repair any breach made in the old," but is in actuality quite impervious to reason.[57] The pretense of argument frequently proves a mask for strategy aimed at shoring up power. This sort of thing makes revolutionary collective action deeply attractive to many women in many different circumstances. And indeed, in many parts of the world, women have to at least some extent advanced their well-being through alliance with Marxist movements. It is beyond my scope here to give an account of when it is acceptable to use illiberal means for liberal ends, or to give advice to women who are faced (as for example in contemporary Afghanistan) with the choice between religious fundamentalism and Marxist collectivism, or (as in contemporary Poland) between traditionalist religious parties and Marxist parties. Even in the United States and Britain, the repeated experience of male irrationality may legitimately cause many feminists to find liberal politics insufficiently radical. To one who repeatedly contends against opposition of the sort Mill describes, the desire to wipe the slate clean of such entrenched obstacles and to begin anew can seem deeply attractive. I wish to note only two things: first, that in the long run it is unlikely that liberal ends will be effectively served by collectivist means—as women in China have had ample occasion to note; second, that any noble ideal can be used as a screen by those who wish to do harm. The right response is to blame and expose the abusers, not to discard the ideal.

Abstraction and Concrete Reality

Closely related to the feminist critique of liberal individualism is the criticism that liberalism's vision of persons is too abstract. By thinking of individuals in ways that sever them from their history and their social context, liberal thinkers have deprived themselves of crucial insights. I believe that there are two different criticisms here. The first has great power, but can be addressed within liberalism; the second is a genuine attack upon liberalism but does not give us a good reason to reject liberalism.

The first attack is pressed by Catharine MacKinnon, Alison Jaggar, and a number of other feminist thinkers.[58] Their claim is that liberalism's disregard of differences between persons that are a product of history and social setting makes it adopt an unacceptably formal conception of equality, one that cannot in the end treat individuals as equals, given the reality of social hierarchy and unequal power. Notice that if this were so, that would be an extremely serious *internal* criticism of liberalism, whose central goal is to show equal respect for persons despite actual differences of power. What do these feminist critics have in mind?

It seems plausible that the liberal principle of formally equal treatment, equality under the law, may, if it is applied in an excessively abstract or remote manner, end up failing to show equal respect for persons. For example, one might use basically liberal language to justify schooling children of different races in separate schools: so long as the schools are equal, the children have been treated as equal; and if any disadvantage attaches to the separation, it is an equal disadvantage to them both. This, in fact, was the reasoning of Herbert Wechsler in a famous article critical of the reasoning in *Brown vs. Board of Education*, the landmark school-desegregation case.[59] Insisting on abstraction for reasons of liberal equality and neutrality, Wechsler held that the introduction into evidence of the history of racial stigmatization and inequality was illegitimate, and could only result in a biased judgment "tailored to the immediate result." Similar reasoning has been used in cases involving gender. In a 1994 sexual harassment case brought by the first woman to work in the tinsmith shop in the General Motors plant in Indiana, the lower court judge, abstracting from the asymmetry of power between Carr and her male coworkers, held that the continual use of obscenities toward Carr by the male workers was exactly the same as the occasional use of a four-letter word by Carr: both reflected only the "ribald banter of the tinsmith's shop." Judge Posner, overruling the lower court judge on the findings of fact, held that the asymmetry of power—including its social meaning in historical terms—was a crucial part of the facts of the case.[60] Their use of language was harassing and intimidating in a way that hers could not be. If liberal neutrality forbids one to take cognizance of such facts, this would indeed be a grave difficulty for liberalism.

In general, liberalism has sometimes been taken to require that the law be "sex-blind," behaving as if the social reality before us were a neutral starting point, and refusing to recognize ways in which the status quo embodies historical asymmetries of power. Feminists have worried, for example, that this sort of neutrality will prevent them from demanding pregnancy and maternity leaves as parts of women's equality of opportunity.[61] Many feminists support a variety of affirmative action programs based on women's history of disadvantage and subordination. If liberal feminism would prevent the government of Bangladesh from investing its money disproportionately in literacy programs aimed at women, or in job training programs for women, this would lose liberalism the regard of most thinkers about women in international politics—including not only leading feminists such as Catharine MacKinnon, who is commonly described as a radical, but including also Gary Becker, who, in his column in *Business Week* has argued for government support for female literacy in connection with global population control. In short, to a wide range of thinkers, formal neutrality of an abstract sort makes little sense, when one is confronted with entrenched asymmetries of power.[62]

It seems to me mistaken, however, to think that liberalism has ever been committed to this type of unrealistic and ahistorical abstraction.[63] MacKinnon is absolutely correct to think that some liberal legal thinkers, and some important Supreme Court decisions, have been guilty of this error; her critique of liberal equality theory is a valuable and correct critique of positions that have been influential in the law. But liberal philosophers have, on the whole, seen more deeply—and, I would say, more consistently—when they have rejected the purely formal notion of equality. Liberals standardly grant that the equality of opportunity that individuals have a right to demand from their governments has material prerequisites, and that these prerequisites may vary depending on one's situation in society. One way of putting this that Amartya Sen and I have favored is to say that liberalism aims at creating equality *of capabilities*, meaning that the aim is not just to distribute some resources around, but also to see that they truly go to work in promoting the capacity of people to choose a life in accordance with their own thinking.[64] We think that the sort of liberalism best equipped to handle this task is one that might be called "perfectionist liberalism" in the sense that it is slightly less neutral about what human functions are important and valuable than is classical Kantian liberalism.[65] The differences between our view and Rawls's on this issue are highly subtle, however, and squarely within the mainstream liberal tradition.[66]

More important for our present purposes, even Rawls, with his great care not to bring any definite conception of the good into the formulation of society's basic structure, nonetheless provides political thought with ample resources to think well about difference and hierarchy. He insists very strongly on a distinction between merely formal equal liberty and what he calls the "equal worth of liberty," and also between formal equality of opportunity and truly fair equality of opportunity; the latter members of each pair have material prerequisites that are likely to involve redistribution. The parties in Rawls's original position do not know what group they themselves belong to; but they know all pertinent general facts about economics, politics, and human psychology, and presumably facts about race and gender relations would be among such general facts. The general principles they will choose will guarantee the equal worth of the various liberties and fully fair equality of opportunity to members of disadvantaged groups. In applying those principles at the constitutional and legislative phases, with fuller information, they would certainly judge that "separate but equal" schools did not, given the history of race relations, guarantee fair equality of opportunity.[67] Noting that women ubiquitously face special hurdles on the way to becoming equal, they could insist on allocating special resources to women's equality, whether through education or in other ways. They would do so in the name of equality itself, viewing it as a violation of equality not to do so.

Liberals will continue to differ about the topic of differential treatment, especially in the area of affirmative action. Libertarian liberals allow wide latitude for advantages that individuals derive from morally irrelevant attributes of birth and social location, but they are strict on the rules that should govern benefits, insisting on a type of neutrality in which morally irrelevant characteristics play no role in the design of distributive policies and programs. Rawlsian liberals, noting that individuals arrive in society with many advantages that they have already derived from morally irrelevant characteristics, think it not just reasonable but morally required to readjust things in order that individuals should not be kings and princes; they therefore permit themselves a more extensive scrutiny of the history of group hierarchy and subordination, rejecting abstractness at this point as incompatible with a fully equal treatment. Feminist liberals have typically followed this strand of liberal thinking to at least some extent,[68] and their criticisms of other ideas of neutrality have been very important in generating legal change.

The criticism, then, is a serious criticism of some parts of the liberal political and legal tradition, and of the obtusely remote language this tradition has sometimes chosen to characterize human affairs; but it can be and frequently has been accommodated within liberalism. To address it well, liberalism needs to pay close attention to history, and to the narratives of people who are in situations of inequality. This it will do best if, in the spirit of Rousseau's *Émile*, it allows a generous role for the imagination in the formulation and the writing of liberal theory.[69]

Another criticism of liberal abstractness cuts deeper.[70] Many communitarian thinkers, among them some feminists, have held that liberalism's determination to think of persons in abstraction from allegedly morally irrelevant features, such as birth, class, ethnicity, gender, religion, and race, entails a pernicious form of "essentialism" that disregards the extent to which people are deeply identified with their religious heritage, their ethnicity, and so forth, and the extent to which these social and historical differences shape people. In one sense, we could say again that this is just a mistake: Liberalism is very interested in knowing these historical facts of difference, precisely in order to ensure fair equality of opportunity.[71] But there is a deep point that is correct: liberalism does think that the core of rational and moral personhood is something all human beings share, shaped though it may be in different ways by their differing social circumstances. And it does give this core a special salience in political thought, defining the public realm in terms of it, purposefully refusing the same salience in the public political conception to differences of gender and rank and class and religion.[72] This, of course, does not mean that people may not choose to identify themselves with their religion or ethnicity or gender, and to make that identification absolutely central in their lives. But for the liberal, that fact of choice is the essential fact; politics can take these features into account only in ways that are carefully structured in order to preserve respect for choice. This does not mean that these features of people's lives are treated as unimportant; indeed, in the case of religion it is because they are regarded as so important that any imposition on a person's conscience on these matters would be utterly inappropriate in the public political conception.[73]

At this point deep conflicts arise between liberalism and various religious and traditional views of life, insofar as the latter hold that freedom of choice is not a central ethical goal. Even if those views are accommodated respectfully within a liberal polity, their adherents may feel that respectful accommodation within a regime of toleration and free choice is not accommodation enough. Many delicate legal and political issues arise at this point. I shall not pursue them here.

The more urgent question for our purposes is, What values prized by feminists are likely to be slighted in this liberal emphasis upon choice? If women are understood to be, first and foremost, members of families, or members of religious traditions, or even members of ethnic groups—rather than, first and foremost, as human centers of choice and freedom—is this likely to be in any way better for women than is the "abstract individualism" of liberalism? Better in whose terms? we have to ask, and of course we will encounter at this point many religious women who sincerely hold that the account of their identity given in the Laws of Manu[74] or the *Analects* of Confucius or the Qu'ran, or whatever, is superior vis à vis their flourishing to the account given in Kant and Mill. We cannot follow out all those lines of argument here—although we should note that all such views group people under abstract universal categories, and therefore cannot consistently attack liberalism for its own use of an abstract universal.[75]

But we can ask to what extent the same feminists who criticize liberalism for its abstractness can, in all consistency, jettison the liberal account of the human essence in favor of an account that gives more centrality to "accidental" features of religion or class or even gender. For these features are especially likely not to have been chosen by the women themselves and to embody views of life that devalue and subordinate them. Even feminists who are themselves communitarians should be skeptical about accepting uncritically this feature of communitarian thought. Communitarianism need not be altogether uncritical of the status quo, and feminist communitarians can certainly avail themselves of liberal principles when criticizing an unjust social order.[76] But feminists such as Jaggar and MacKinnon, who are generally critical of communitarian thought out of their concern for fundamental social change, should be especially skeptical of communitarian anti-essentialism. The idea that all human beings have a core of moral personhood that exerts claims on government, no matter what the world has done to it, is an idea that the women of the world badly need to vindicate their own equality and to argue for political and social change. If one thinks of a woman as just what the world has made of her and that all existing distinctions are of equal moral relevance, one loses a grip on why this making is unjust. It is the disparity between humanity and its social deformation that gives rise to claims of justice. And the communitarian vision of persons, in which we are at heart and essentially what our traditions have made us, is a vision that leaves little scope for the type of critique of institutions and customs that feminists such as Jaggar and MacKinnon wish to make.[77]

One may make one further reply to feminists who stress the importance of recognizing differences of race and class. This is that the liberal approach is a principled approach that addresses itself to issues of human dignity in a completely general way. As a liberal feminist, one is also, by the entailment of one's very feminist position, also an antiracist, a defender of religious toleration, and a supporter of fair equality of opportunity. One's feminism is not mere identity politics, putting the interests of women as such above the interests of other marginalized groups. It is part of a systematic and justifiable program that addresses exclusion and marginalization across the board in the name of human dignity. To that extent, the liberal feminist is in a better position than are many other feminists to show her fellow women that she has not neglected legitimate claims that are peculiar to their own class- or religion- or race-based identities.

As Onora O'Neill aptly says: feminism needs abstractness without idealization.[78] What she means by this is that feminism needs to operate with a general notion of the human core, without forgetting that this core has been differently situated and also shaped in different times and places. We should not overlook the questions raised by these differences, and we cannot formulate a just social policy if we do. But insofar as feminism cuts more deeply against liberalism, denying the salience and value of the whole idea of the human core, it gives up something vital to the most powerful feminist arguments.[79]

Reason and Emotion

Liberalism traditionally holds that human beings are above all reasoning beings and that the dignity of reason is the primary source of human equality. As Jaggar puts it, "Liberal political theory is grounded on the conception of human beings as essentially rational agents."[80] Here liberal thinkers are not alone: they owe much to their forebears in the Western philosophical tradition, in particular the Greek and Roman Stoics, whose conception of the dignity of reason as a source of equal human worth profoundly influenced Kant, Adam Smith, John Rawls, and others as well. Continuing the Stoic heritage, liberalism typically holds that the relevant type of reason is practical reason, the capacity for understanding moral distinctions, for ranking and evaluating options, for selecting means to ends, and for planning a life. Thinkers have differed in the relative weight they assign to these different components, but not in their choice of practical over theoretical reasoning power as the essential mark of humanity.

Modern feminist thinkers usually grant that this liberal move has had at least some value for women in seeking to secure their equality. They point out that earlier feminists, from Cartesian philosopher Mary Astell to Mary Wollstonecraft, were able to appeal to women's rational capacity as a ground for claims to full political and moral equality. (They could indeed go much further back in history to support this claim: for Astell's arguments are closely related to the arguments of first-century Stoic Musonius Rufus, in his treatises "That Women Too Should Do Philosophy" and "Should Sons and Daughters Have the Same Education?")[81] And they could reflect that the decision to base moral and political claims on an innate capacity of individuals, rather than on social endowments or positions or relations, is certainly one that opens the door to radical claims of empowerment for the disempowered, who can now say that they are the equals of kings, no matter where they are currently placed in society. Noam Chomsky forcefully made this point long ago, defending the radical potential of rationalism and arguing for its superiority to various forms of empiricism and historical determinism.[82]

On the other hand, feminists have worried that liberalism is far too rationalist: that by placing all emphasis on reason as a mark of humanity, it has emphasized a trait that males traditionally prize and denigrated traits, such as sympathy and emotion and imagination, that females traditionally prize. This emphasis has permitted men to denigrate women for their emotional natures, and to marginalize them on account of their alleged lack of reason. This would not have been possible, the argument goes, had political philosophy been grounded in a conception that gave, at least, equal weight to reason and to emotion.

Most feminists who make such claims do not argue for innate differences between the sexes, although some do.[83] Their argument is, more frequently, that women, as a result of their experiences of mothering and in general of family love and care, have rightly valued some important elements in human life that men frequently undervalue.[84] Liberal philosophy is accused of making that common male error, in a way that frequently contributes to the denigration of women.

This is a complicated issue, since grappling with it fully would require us to argue for an account of what emotions are. The objection, as I have stated it, assumed that emotions are not forms of thought or reasoning, that there is a strong contrast to be drawn between reason and emotion. But is this true? Both the history of philosophy and contemporary psychological inquiry contain much debate on precisely that issue. On the whole, the dominant view, both in the Western philosophical tradition and in recent work in cognitive psychology is that emotions such as fear, anger, compassion, and grief involve evaluative appraisals that are full of imaginative and mental activity, appraisals in which the person (or animal) surveys the objects and persons in the world around him with an eye to how important goals and projects are doing. If one holds some such view of what emotions involve, then the entire distinction between reason and emotion begins to be called into question, and one can no longer assume that a thinker who focuses on reason is by that very move excluding emotion, or vice versa.[85] So we must proceed cautiously here, looking both at the view of the emotion-reason contrast a thinker holds and also at the normative judgments the thinker makes about how good or valuable emotions are. This is tricky, because in the liberal tradition these positions cut across one another: thinkers who hold a strong form of the emotion-reason contrast disagree about the value they attach to emotions, as do thinkers who consider emotions to involve thought and evaluation. By trying to keep these distinctions straight we can make some progress in understanding the force of the feminist objections.

First, then, we do discover in the liberal tradition some philosophers who conceive of emotions as impulses distinct from reason, unintelligent forces that push the personality around. On this basis, they do endorse a contrast between reason and emotion. Kant and Hume are very different examples of this contrast. One strong feminist objection against elements in the liberal tradition is the objection that this is an implausible and ultimately indefensible picture of what emotions are.[86] To put a complex issue very briefly, it is implausible because it neglects the extent to which perceptions of an object and beliefs about the object are an intrinsic part of the experience of a complex emotion such as grief or fear. Grief, for example, is not simply a tug at the heart-strings: it involves the perception of an enormous void in the subject's life, and the belief that an object of great importance has been lost. Emotions involve ways of seeing.[87] This objection has been made by all sorts of philosophers and psychologists independently of feminist concerns; but the feminist version of the objection suggests that the philosophers who put forward such a picture have been insufficiently reflective about the nature of emotional experience, and that this failure to look closely at experience may derive from a cultural suspiciousness of emotions that is frequently distributed along gender lines.[88]

But even Kant and Hume, whatever the deficiencies in their analysis of emotions, are far from dismissing emotions from their normative picture of the moral life. Kant is guarded about the contribution of emotions to moral motivation, but even he sees a necessary role for pity in motivating benevolence; Hume sees the emotions as the source of all the ends that morality pursues. Modern feminist Annette Baier has recently defended Hume's conception of the passions as the one feminists ought to use.[89] Although I am far from agreeing with Baier, since I think Hume's conception indefensible,[90] I think she is right to acknowledge the central place Hume gives to passion in his account of human nature. So even if major liberal thinkers have failed to appreciate sufficiently the amount of intelligence involved in emotion, this has not altogether stopped them from valuing the contribution of emotion to our moral choices.

Let me now turn to the cognitive conceptions of emotion. Quite a few philosophers who focus on reason, and who make reason a hallmark of the human, have, in fact, a strongly cognitive conception of emotion, and think of emotions as activities of the rational faculty. Among these philosophers are some ancestors of liberalism, such as the Stoics and Spinoza. The Stoics and Spinoza dislike the emotions intensely; they do so, however, not on the grounds that emotions are not reason-based, but because they believe that the emotions involve false or confused reasoning, appraisals that ascribe to persons and things outside our own control more importance for our well-being than they actually possess. They hold this because of their normative views about individual self-sufficiency, which we have already discussed; these views are not widely shared in the liberal tradition. Feminists have suggested that these views derive from a male suspiciousness of all attachments.[91] Whether or not there is truth in this suggestion, the Stoic anti-emotion position is certainly defended with other arguments as well, having to do with the containment of aggression and jealousy, and should be criticized with these arguments squarely in view.

But for those who reject those arguments, liberalism offers other resources. The position that many feminists would seem to favor, as doing most justice to women's experience of the value of emotional attachment and connection, would be a position that first analyzes emotions as containing cognition and then evaluates them positively, as having at least some value in the ethical life. This position is powerfully represented in the liberal tradition—to some extent under the influence of Aristotle, who influentially held such a position. Both Jean-Jacques Rousseau and Adam Smith seem to have held that emotions involve thought and imagination; they also hold that the capacity for sympathy is a central mark of both private and public rationality, and indeed of humanity as such. Rousseau holds that a person who has no capacity for feeling pain at the distress of others is not fully human, that this capacity for imaginative response is the essential thing that draws us together in community and makes political thought possible in the first place. Smith's entire account of the "judicious spectator"—his model of good public judgment—is preoccupied with ascertaining the correct balance in the passions of anger and sympathy and love that such a public actor will feel. These positions seem to be independent of their views about women's political role, which are remarkably conventional and nonprogressive; nonetheless, they appear to be positions that offer what feminists have demanded. To this list we may certainly add Mill, whose *Autobiography* provides a moving testament to the barrenness of a rationality starved of emotional attachment and imaginative stimulation.

What, then, is the issue? What does this liberal tradition assert about emotions, that feminist thinkers might still wish to deny? The liberal tradition agrees that emotions should not be trusted as guides to life without being subjected to some sort of critical scrutiny. They are thought to be only as reliable as the evaluations they contain; and since such evaluations of objects are frequently absorbed from society, from its pictures of honor and status and worth, they will be only as reliable as those social norms. To naturalize them would be to naturalize the status quo. In general, emotions, like other forms of thought and imagination, should be valued as elements in a life governed by critical reasoning about what is just and good.

Some feminists, however, hold that this entire idea of subjecting emotion to rational appraisal is mistaken, an imposition of a male norm of cool rationality on the natural vigor and intensity of the passions. Unlike other feminist objections to liberal views of reason and emotion—which, as I have argued, are not accurate as directed against the strongest liberal positions—this one directly assails a central tenet of liberalism. Nel Noddings, a prominent proponent of this objection in her influential book *Caring*,[92] holds that women's experience of mothering reveals a rich terrain of emotional experience into which judgment and appraisal do not and should not enter. For example, there is a primitive bond of joy and love between mother and child that would be sullied by reflection, and this primitive unscrutinized love should be the model for our social attachments. From the perspective of a moral view such as Noddings's, liberalism, by urging people to ask whether their emotions are appropriate, robs moral life of a spontaneous movement toward others that is at the very core of morality.[93] Unless we give ourselves away to others without asking questions, we have not behaved in a fully moral way. It is the very unreasoning and unjudicious character of maternal love and care that make it a fitting paradigm for social life.

Noddings appeals, here, to images of selfless giving that lie deep in the Jewish and Christian traditions, though her view would certainly be controversial in both.[94] Noddings holds that her maternal paradigm of care is incompatible with norms of reflective caring that are preferred by liberalism. And Noddings is correct. The liberal tradition is profoundly opposed, at its heart, to the idea that people should spontaneously give themselves away without reflection, judgment, or reciprocity. At last, then, we have identified a position about the emotional life that is truly opposed to liberalism; it puts itself forward as a feminist position, since it appeals to maternal experience as a paradigm for all human concern. Liberalism says, let them give themselves away to others—provided that they so choose in all freedom. Noddings says that this is one thought too many—that love based on reflection lacks some of the spontaneity and moral value of true maternal love.

What should feminists say about this? First of all, I think, we should ask a good number of questions about Noddings's claim that maternal love and joy can and should be innocent of appraisal and judgment. She gives an example that makes at least one mother doubt.

> There is the joy that unaccountably floods over me as I walk into the house and see my daughter asleep on the sofa. She is exhausted from basketball playing, and her hair lies curled on a damp forehead. The joy I feel is immediate.... There is a feeling of connectedness in my joy, but no awareness of a particular belief and, certainly, no conscious assessment.[95]

Noddings concludes that such moments, in which consciousness is emptied of focus and the personality simply flows toward another in a condition of fusion, lie at the core of moral motivation.

Let us consider this allegedly thoughtless and objectless joy. Noddings thinks nothing; she simply basks in the fused experience of maternal caring.[96] But can it really be the case that she has no thoughts at all? Doesn't Noddings have to have, in fact, the belief that her daughter is alive and asleep on the couch, rather than dead? Change that belief, and her emotion would change from joy to devastating grief. She may not have to stop to ponder such a fact, but when her daughter was a baby she probably did.[97] Again, doesn't her joy presuppose the recognition that it is her daughter there on the couch rather than a burglar who has broken in? Doesn't its intensity also presuppose a recognition of the central importance of her daughter in her life? To some extent, then, the view seems just wrong of the case as characterized. But to the extent to which Noddings does give in to a joy without thought, how wise is she to do so? It does not occur to her, for example, to ask whether her daughter is sleeping from a drug or alcohol overdose, or following risky sex with a boyfriend, or sexual abuse from a relative. Assuming things are as she thinks, her joy is fine, and her maternal reactions morally appropriate. But aren't there circumstances in which the erasure of thought (which, as we see, is not complete even in this example) could be pushed a little too far? If her daughter really is sleeping from a heroin overdose or is unconscious from sexual abuse, Noddings's joy would be inappropriate and her maternal responses harmful. Such heedless caring is dangerous in a world where many of the forces affecting the lives of children are malign. Noddings may live in a world in which she may safely bracket those concerns, but most mothers do not. As Nietzsche wrote in a related connection: blessed are the sleepy ones—for they shall soon nod off.[98]

A child is not an arm or a leg or a wish, but a separate person. This person lives in a world full of both delight and danger. This means that the mother had better think, and it means that she had better teach her child how to think. And she had better think critically, asking whether the norms and traditions embodied in the emotions of fear and shame and honor in her society—and in her own emotions as well—are reasonable or unreasonable norms. What shall she teach her child to fear and what, not to fear? How shall she urge her child to see the stranger who offers her an ice cream, or the teacher who caresses her, or the friend who says that people with black skin are bad? Unless society is perfect, as it probably is not, critical thought needs to inform emotional development and response if caring is to produce good citizens. The suggestion of Smith and Rousseau that emotional responses should be scrutinized for their appropriateness to their object, and cultivated as parts of a life organized by reason, seems a better recipe for maternal care than Noddings's emphasis on thoughtless giving.

Even were symbiotic fused caring a good thing in the mother-child relationship, a very different sort of care seems required in the political life. Here indiscriminate self-giving-away seems a very bad idea, especially for women, who have frequently been brought up to think that they should sacrifice their well-being to others without demanding anything for themselves. This has frequently served male interests and harmed women. We should not naturalize the status quo. A little reflection, far from representing "one thought too many,"[99] might provide the saving distance between social norms and one's own selfhood. In short, Noddings and her allies risk turning some of the pathologies of women's lives into virtues. Even in the family there is no reason why women should simply give themselves away without demanding a just distribution of resources.

Recall, now, the widows at the conference in Bangalore. Having spent most of their lives thinking of themselves as mere adjuncts of a family, with no rights and no separate identity, they started to learn not to give themselves away without thinking. And this seemed to be a good thing. The women themselves were delighted with their newfound self-expression and freedom, and the expansion in their set of choices itself seems a definite good. But still, we might ask: aren't these women being brainwashed by these liberal ideas? The widows in Bangalore gathered under the auspices of regional development workers and international activists, who had some pretty definite goals in mind, liberal goals. The *Hindu* article reports that the women were "urged" to think of themselves in a certain way; Noddings would presumably object that this way of thinking involves giving up a valuable kind of organic unity within the family that women had previously prized. Indian feminist Veena Das develops a similar position, arguing that the notion of personal welfare is alien to Indian women.[100] If a typical Indian rural woman were to be asked about her personal "welfare," Das claims, she would find the question unintelligible, except as a question about how the whole family is doing. The thinking of these women, Das holds, exemplifies a valuable type of emotional devotion, which will be destroyed by the heavy hand of liberal individualism.

Here we must distinguish several different aspects of these women's familial devotion. Liberal individualism, I have argued, does not ask a woman to become an egoist, putting her own gratification first and other people's second. So far as liberalism is concerned, she may be (and in most versions ought to be) a committed altruist, even to the point of making considerable sacrifices of her own personal welfare for the sake of others. Nor, so far as liberalism is concerned, need she be dedicated to self-sufficiency, to minimizing her attachments to and needs from others. Again, she may continue to place friendship and love squarely at the heart of her plan. What liberalism asks, however, is that the woman *distinguish* the question of her own well-being from the question of the well-being of others, and notice what tensions might exist between the two, even if they are, as so often they are, bound up in one another. Liberalism asks, further, that a woman reflect and choose for herself the extent to which she will indeed sacrifice her own well-being for others—that she do so not out of habit or convention, but as the result of an individual decision, freely made. It is of course a large matter to spell out the conditions under which such choices would count as freely made, but we can at least agree that many conditions under which women make sacrifices (such as conditions of malnutrition, intimidation, lack of education, and lack of political power) are not such conditions. It is common for people to internalize the roles society gives them and to act unreflectively in accordance with these roles. People also adjust their desires and preferences to what is possible, so that they may even in a limited sense be content with their lot. But in circumstances of traditional hierarchy and limited information, we surely should not assume that the sacrifices of well-being a woman makes are freely chosen, whatever account of free choice and autonomy we ultimately prefer. And this does seem to matter. As Rousseau and Smith and Mill would advise: let her love others and give herself away—provided that she does so freely and judiciously, with the proper critical scrutiny of the relevant social norms. I believe that this proposal, far from killing love through excessive male rationality, indicates the conditions under which love is a healthy part of a flourishing life.[101]

In fact, the most powerful criticism that feminists have made against liberal views of reason and emotion goes, I believe, in exactly the opposite direction from Noddings's proposal. This criticism, made most influentially by Catharine MacKinnon and Andrea Dworkin, and by now commonly accepted in at least some form, is that emotion, desire, and preference are not given or "natural" but powerfully shaped by social norms and appraisals—and that many emotions of both men and women are shaped by social norms that subordinate women to men.[102] MacKinnon has powerfully argued that not only male aggression and female timidity, but also the character of both male and female sexual desire, are often powerfully influenced by the social norm that women ought to be the subordinates of men. Men eroticize domination and learn to achieve sexual satisfaction in connection with its assertion. Women come to eroticize submission and learn to find satisfaction by giving themselves away. This, MacKinnon has argued, is a profound detriment both to individuals and to society.

MacKinnon's insistence on recognizing and criticizing socially deformed preferences goes against one strand in contemporary liberalism, namely, that part of economic utilitarianism that has standardly taken preferences as given, as a stable bedrock to which law and economics respond, rather than as material that is itself shaped by law and economics. Economists are now increasingly calling such views into question.[103] Such views have always been profoundly at odds with the Kantian liberal tradition, which insists that individuals' desires are frequently distorted by self-interest. They are even more clearly at odds with the liberalisms of Adam Smith and Rousseau, both of whom were preoccupied with the criticism of diseased emotions and desires, and who saw bad social arrangements as at the core of those diseases. Rousseau powerfully shows how differences of rank corrupt human sympathy, preventing nobles from seeing their own pain in the pain they inflict on a peasant.[104] Smith shows how the importance attached by society to money and status corrupt emotions of anger, love, and sympathy, producing people who are far from good citizens or good moral agents.[105] Both follow the ancient Stoic tradition, according to which human beings are naturally good, and what is envious and malicious and aggressive in them results from social deformation.[106]

Nor are such insights at all foreign to the utilitarian tradition itself. Mill prominently recognized the social deformation of preferences, especially with regard to sex roles. Women, he held, internalize their inferior status in ways that shape their desires and choice, and many of these ways are very damaging to them and to society. He held that "what is now called the nature of women is an eminently artificial thing—the result of forced repression in some directions, unnatural stimulation in others." It is, he says, as if one had grown a tree half in a vapor bath and half in the snow, and then, noting that one part of it is withered and another part luxuriant, had held that it was the nature of the tree to be that way.[107] Men also find their desires shaped by the experience of domination. They become arrogant and overweening and malicious—again, in ways that are bad, both for them and for society. Mill draws special attention to the way in which society eroticizes female "meekness, submissiveness and resignation of all individual will" as "an essential part of sexual attractiveness," whereas strength of will is eroticized in the case of men.[108] Given the upbringing of women, it would be "a miracle if the object of being attractive to men had not become the polar star of feminine education and formation of character,"[109] and equally miraculous if this object had not been understood to entail subordination. Here again, Mill makes a judicious comparison to feudalism: To both nobles and vassals, domination and subordination seemed natural, and the desires of both were shaped by this sense of the natural. Equality always seems unnatural to the dominator, and this is why any departure from women's subjection to men appears unnatural. "But how entirely, even in this case, the feeling is dependent on custom, appears by ample experience."[110]

What is new and remarkable in the work of MacKinnon and Dworkin is the insight that even sexual desire—which has often been thought to be natural and presocial, even by thinkers who would not hold this of envy and fear and anger[111]—has a social shaping, and that this shaping is often far from benign. Their central idea is already present in Mill, but they have developed it much further and given it shape and power, partly on account of the opportunity they have to discuss sexual matters with a candor unavailable to Mill. One may differ with many of their analyses and normative conclusions; but it seems hard to avoid granting that they have identified a phenomenon of immense human importance, one that lies at the heart of a great deal of human misery. Insofar as liberalism has left the private sphere unexamined, this critique of desire is a critique of liberalism. It challenges liberalism to do for desire what it has often done with greed and anger and envy—that is, to conduct a rigorous examination of the social formation of erotic longing and to think of the moral education of children with these aims in mind. As Mill shows us, such critical scrutiny of desire is right in line with liberalism's deepest aspirations.

Doesn't this ruin sex? As in the case of maternal caring, so here: Doesn't the liberal ask women to have "one thought too many?" Doesn't sex at its best involve a heedless giving away of oneself to the other, an erasing of conscious reflection? Yes and no. Liberal feminism—and here I believe it is right to treat MacKinnon as a kind of Kantian liberal, inspired by a deep vision of personhood and autonomy[112]—does not ask women not to abandon themselves to and in pleasure, any more than it asks them not to invest themselves deeply in caring for children and loved ones. Once again, however, it says: fine, so long as you think first. Abandon yourself, so long as you do so within a context of equality and noninstrumental respect.[113] In some areas of life, perhaps, noninstrumental respect can be taken for granted. In this one, because of its history of distortion, it cannot be, and so you must think. If, as Mill plausibly suggests, "the generality of the male sex cannot yet tolerate the idea of living with an equal,"[114] this thinking will occasion tension, upheaval, and pain. The liberal holds that this pain should be risked rather than endure the hidden pain that arises from subordination and the passions it shapes.

In short, wherever you most mistrust habit, there you have the most need for reason. Women have lots of grounds to mistrust most habits people have had through the centuries, just as Rousseau's poor people have reason to mistrust the moral emotions of kings. This means that women have an especially great need for reason. Males can at least take consolation from the thought that the habits they live by have been formed by them, whether for good or for ill. Women should recognize that where the voice of tradition speaks, that voice is most often male, and it has even invented a little squeaky voice for women to speak in, a voice that may be far from being their own true voice, whatever precise content we attach to that idea. As MacKinnon says of Carol Gilligan's concept of the "different voice" of women: If you will take your foot off our necks, then you will see in what voice women speak.[115]

In an age skeptical of reason, as Mill rightly argues, we have a hard time unmasking such deeply habitual fictions. Thus the romantic reaction against reason that he saw in his own time seemed to him profoundly subversive of any reform that goes against deeply seated custom. "For the apotheosis of Reason," he concludes, "we have substituted that of Instinct; and we call everything instinct which we find in ourselves and for which we cannot trace any rational foundation." Contemporary feminism should beware of making the same mistake.[116]

Two things fill the mind with ever-increasing awe, wrote Kant: "The starry sky above me, and the moral law within me."[117] In that famous statement we see the radical vision of liberalism. Think what real people usually hold in awe: money, power, success, nice clothes, fancy cars, the dignity of kings, the wealth of corporations, the authority of vassals and lords and despots of all sorts and—perhaps most important of all—the authority of custom and tradition. Think what real women frequently hold in awe, or at least in fear: the physical power of men, the authority of men in the workplace, the sexual allure of male power, the alleged maleness of the deity, the control males have over work and shelter and food. The liberal holds none of these things in awe. She feels reverence for the world, its mystery and its wonder. And she reveres the capacity of persons to choose and fashion a life. That capacity has no gender, so the liberal does not revere distinctions of gender, any more than the dazzling equipment of nobles and kings. Some liberal thinkers have in fact revered established distinctions of gender. But, insofar as they did, they did not follow the vision of liberalism far enough. It is the vision of a beautiful, rich, and difficult world, in which a community of persons regard one another as free and equal but also as finite and needy—and therefore strive to arrange their relations on terms of justice and liberty. In a world governed by hierarchies of power and fashion, this is still, as it was from the first, a radical vision, a vision that can and should lead to social revolution. It is always radical to make the demand to see and to be seen as human, rather than as someone's lord, or someone's subject.

Such demands will not be accepted without struggle. To those who receive them, they bring the threat of loss of privilege, and people will fight to retain their privileges. To those who make them, they bring the threat of exchanging small comforts for large uncertainties. In short, to the women who follow the vision of liberalism and give voice to its demands, it will be likely to bring pain—the pain of change, the pain of social alienation, the pain of personal loneliness. I believe it is best for women to make these demands and to embrace this vision.

Notes

I am extremely grateful to Al Alschuler, Ruth Chang, Richard De Liberty, David Estlund, Elizabeth Garrett, Stephen Holmes, Dan Kahan, Jeremy Bendik Keymer, Tracey Meares, Richard Posner, Kaspar Stoffelmayr, David Strauss, Cass Sunstein, and Candace Vogler for their very helpful comments on an earlier draft, and to Ross Davies for research assistance. This lecture will appear in revised form as chapter 2 of my forthcoming volume, *Sex and Social Justice* (New York: Oxford University Press, 1998).

1. Roop Rekha Verma, "Femininity, Equality, and Personhood" (address delivered to the American Philosophical Association, December 1992); published in *Women, Culture, and Development: A Study of Human Capabilities*, ed. M. Nussbaum and J. Glover (Oxford: Clarendon Press, 1995), pp. 433–443.

2. Nahid Toubia, "Female Genital Mutilation," in *Women's Rights, Human Rights*, ed. Julie Peters and Andrea Wolper (New York: Routledge, 1995), pp. 224–237, at p. 235; reprinted from N. Toubia, *Female Genital Mutilation: A Call for Global Action* (Women, Inc., 1993).

3. *The Hindu*, April 24, 1994.

4. Alison Jaggar, *Feminist Politics and Human Nature* (Totowa, N.J.: Rowman and Allanheld, 1983; reprint, 1988), pp. 47–48. For related views, see also Carole Pateman, *The Problem of Political Obligation: A Critique of Liberal Theory* (Berkeley: University of California Press, 1979); Nancy C.M. Hartsock, *Money, Sex, and Power* (Boston: Northeastern University Press, 1983). An interesting response to some of the criticisms is found in Marilyn Friedman, "Feminism and Modern Friendship," *Ethics* 99 (1989):304–319.

5. Among many treatments of these topics, see the discussion of the issues in Amartya Sen, "Human Rights and Asian Values?" *The New Republic*, July 10/17, 1997, pp. 33–40. See also the exchange between Albie Sachs and Roberto Unger in *Economic and Social Rights and the Right to Health* (Cambridge: Harvard Law School Human Rights Program, 1993), pp. 12 ff.

6. Of course this power needs development; but the basis for human equality is the possession of the potentiality for that development. Even if individuals possess differing degrees of this basic potentiality, we can say that a sufficient condition for equal moral personality is the possession of a certain basic minimum. See "The Basis of Equality," section 77 in John Rawls, *A Theory of Justice* (Cambridge: Harvard University Press, 1971), pp. 504–512, and also my discussion of "basic capabilities" in "Human Capabilities, Female Human Beings," in *Women, Culture, and Development*. This was also the view of the ancient Stoics.

7. See Martha Nussbaum, "Kant and Stoic Cosmopolitanism," *Journal of Political Philosophy* 5 (1997):1–25. Nussbaum's article also appears in *Perpetual Peace: Essays on Kant's Cosmopolitan Ideal*, ed. James Bohmann and Matthias Lutz-Bachmann (Cambridge: MIT Press, 1997), pp. 25–58; also see Julia Annas, *The Morality of Happiness* (New York: Oxford University Press, 1993).

8. This characterization of the essence of the liberal tradition differs sharply from that given in Ronald Dworkin, "Liberalism," in *A Matter of Principle* (Cambridge: Harvard University Press, 1985), pp. 181–204. Dworkin makes neutrality about conceptions of the good the basic core of liberalism, rather than any more

positive ideal. I would hold that to the extent that liberals are neutral about the good, this is explained by the basic intuition about the worth of choice and the respect for the choice-making capacities of the person. Rawls, for example, seems to me to have a far deeper account of the core of liberalism when he begins from an idea of "free and equal moral persons" and derives a measure of neutrality about the good from that idea. See particularly "Kantian Constructivism and Moral Theory," *Journal of Philosophy* 77 (1980):515–572, esp. pp. 521ff., and "The Priority of Right and Ideas of the Good," *Philosophy and Public Affairs* 17 (1988):251–276.

9. This idea is central in both the Kantian and the utilitarian traditions. See the extensive discussion in John Rawls, *A Theory of Justice*, pp. 11–16, 118–130, etc. For its relation to U.S. constitutional law, see Cass R. Sunstein, *The Partial Constitution* (Cambridge: Harvard University Press, 1993).

10. Some libertarian offshoots of liberalism might be charged with having lost that central idea insofar as they validate existing distributions that have morally irrelevant origins. Some liberals will claim that personal talents and capacities other than the moral faculties ought to be counted as part of the core of the person, and thus, insofar as they confer advantage, as not morally irrelevant; this is one source of the gulf between Nozick and Rawls. But some libertarian arguments also validate existing hierarchies of wealth and class; unless they do so by deriving those advantages from the moral rights of persons (as Nozick tries to do), they are by my account illiberal. For a judicious analysis of Nozick's relationship to two strands of the liberal tradition, see Barbara Fried, "Wilt Chamberlain Revisited: Nozick's 'Justice in Transfer' and the Problem of Market-Based Distribution," *Philosophy and Public Affairs* 24 (1995):226–245.

11. Thus there is room for doubt whether classical utilitarianism is not, in the end, illiberal, in the sense that it treats the desires of all persons as fusible into a single system and ignores the salience of the separateness of persons. This is the primary criticism of utilitarianism developed in the Kantian tradition; see, for example, Rawls, *Theory of Justice*, pp. 183–192, 554–559.

12. For some of the opponents, see Stephen Holmes, *The Anatomy of Anti-Liberalism* (Cambridge: Harvard University Press, 1993).

13. Rawls, *A Theory of Justice*; Nozick, *Anarchy, State, and Utopia* (Oxford: Basil Blackwell, 1974). Both understand themselves to be heirs and rival interpreters of the liberal tradition; in characterizing their difference this way I am not saying anything particularly new or surprising. On this point, see the clear account in R. Dworkin, *Men of Ideas*, ed. B. Magee (Oxford: Oxford University Press, 1982). Nozick is clear that his own validation of existing differences of wealth and class depends on an argument from basic rights of self-ownership and just transfer, and that inequalities that cannot be so justified are unacceptable. His deepest difference from Kantian liberalism is his unargued assumption that features of persons other than the basis of their moral powers have moral weight and relevance, features such as talent in sports, physical strength, cleverness, etc.

14. On this distinction, see Henry S. Richardson, *Practical Deliberation of Final Ends* (New York: Cambridge University Press, 1994), pp. 69–86, 209–227.

15. Even in this area, liberals will differ. Thus, for example, in the area of legal regulation of speech, Cass Sunstein's view holds that political speech is the central type that government needs to protect in protecting respect for persons; Joshua Co-

hen argues, in contrast, that artistic speech is also worthy of protection as embodying expressive capacities that are central to personhood. See Sunstein, *Democracy and the Problem of Free Speech* (New York: Free Press, 1993), pp. 17–51, 121–165; J. Cohen, "Freedom of Expression," *Philosophy and Public Affairs* 22 (1993):207–263. Once again, we see here differences not only about strategies to achieve equal respect but, as well, about the more concrete specification of the notions involved, such as personhood and autonomy. On specification with respect to liberal politics, see Richardson, *Practical Deliberation*, pp. 209–227, esp. pp. 218–227.

A note on U.S. politics: In terms of my discussion here, all major positions represented on the U.S. political scene are to at least some degree liberal positions, insofar as they defend the Constitution. The strongest inclinations to antiliberalism can be seen in conservative and communitarian politics, though even these forces are held in check by the Bill of Rights. (Thus, in a recent documentary program on Plato's *Republic* made for the Discovery Channel, William Bennett said that Plato had some very good ideas about the promotion of virtue and the control of art but then immediately said that of course we think that Plato went too far!) Economic libertarians and their opponents (often called "liberals") are, in terms of my argument, rival heirs of the liberal tradition who differ about how equal respect and liberty should be embodied in laws and institutions. Things are confused by the fact that the Republican Party houses both libertarians and antiliberals. The Democratic Party used to contain many socialist antiliberals and still contains numerous communitarian critics of liberalism.

16. Jaggar, *Feminist Politics*, p. 29.

17. Ibid., p. 30.

18. Ibid., p. 40.

19. Ibid., p. 41.

20. This would seem to be the meaning of the claim that "the egoistic model of human nature" is unable to admit "the values of community" (ibid., p. 45).

21. Jaggar appears to grant this in the case of Rawls (Feminist Politics, p. 31), but she insists, nonetheless, that the psychological egoism inherent in liberal theory has left its deforming marks on Rawls's normative theory.

22. Amartya Sen, "Rational Fools: A Critique of the Behavioural Foundations of Economic Theory," in *Choice, Welfare, and Measurement* (Oxford: Basil Blackwell, 1982), pp. 84–108, discussed in Jaggar, *Feminist Politics*, p. 45.

23. See Jaggar, *Feminist Politics*, pp. 31 ff.

24. Although one probably should not count Hobbes as a part of the liberal tradition.

25. Nor is it correct to think that the liberal conception of "happiness" is simply identical to the satisfaction of self-interested desire; there would appear to be no major liberal theorist (with the possible exception of Bentham) of whom that is unqualifiedly true, and in the Kantian tradition there is no tendency at all in this direction.

26. On these arguments, see my *The Therapy of Desire: Theory and Practice in Hellenistic Ethics* (Princeton: Princeton University Press, 1994), especially chaps. 11–13.

27. See Mill, "On Liberty," in *Utilitarianism, On Liberty and Considerations on Representative Government* (London: J. M. Dent, 1972), pp. 114–131, where he speaks of the importance of overcoming people's lack of interest in the world and getting them engaged in life.

28. We may remark that ancient proponents of self-sufficiency favored masturbation as a way of minimizing dependency on others; see Diogenes Laertius *Life of Diogenes the Cynic* 6.45 and 6.69; for Kant, masturbation is the "most disgraceful and the most degrading" conduct "of which man is capable." See his *Lectures on Ethics*, trans. Louis Infield (Indianapolis: Hackett, 1963), p. 170. Whatever we may think about this strange judgment, it is surely not that of a person who promotes self-sufficiency above all else.

29. In these remarks about Buddhism I am much indebted to conversation with Paul Griffiths.

30. Thus I find quite puzzling Jaggar's claim that liberalism rejects human embodiment (pp. 31, 40–42). One might, of course, have a metaphysic of separate substances without making embodiment central to it, but then it would be difficult to explain why liberalism would devote so much attention to the feeding of those substances.

31. Putting things in terms of happiness and misery should not be taken to suggest either that liberalism is not critical of existing preferences and desires or that the liberal emphasis on separateness requires Pareto optimality for all policies. It might well be that we will allow a larger amount of happiness for Q to compensate for a larger amount of misery for X, if we judge that X's self-generated taste for luxury and power is at the root of his misery.

32. For these statistics, see Nussbaum, introduction to *Women, Culture, and Development*; they are taken from the UNDP *Human Development Report* 1993 and from J. Drèze and A. Sen, *Hunger and Public Action* (Oxford: Clarendon Press, 1989).

33. *Human Development Report* 1995 (New York: United Nations Development Program, 1995), p. 44.

34. For these two statistics, and many others, see *The World's Women, 1970–1990: Trends and Statistics* (New York: United Nations, 1991), pp. 19–22.

35. See Lori L. Heise, "Freedom Close to Home: The Impact of Violence Against Women on Reproductive Rights," in *Women's Rights, Human Rights*, pp. 238–255, citing M. Isabel Rosas, "Violencia Sexual y Politica Criminal," CLADEM Informativo No. 6, Lima, April 1992; Tatiana Treguear L. and Carmen Carro B., *Ninas Madres: Recuiento de una Experiencia* (San Jose, Costa Rica: PROCAL, 1991); and Elizabeth Shrader-Cox, "Violence Against Women in Central America and Its Impact on Reproductive Health" (paper presented at the Safe Motherhood Central America Conference, Guatemala City, January 27–31, 1992). One should note that women in these societies are not secluded, so the high proportion in the Costa Rican example is significant.

36. See, for example, Heise, "Freedom Close to Home," supra note 27 at pp. 243–244; Department of State, *Country Reports on Human Rights Practices for 1994* (Comm. Print 1995) (Switzerland criminalized marital rape in 1992); ibid., p. 809 (a 1994 Finnish statute equated marital rape and nonmarital rape); "Marital Rape Offence," *The [London] Times*, June 15, 1994 (marital rape became a common law crime in England in 1991); "Sri Lanka Tightens Laws to Guard Women, Children," *Inter Press Service*, September 29, 1995 (a new statute criminalizes marital rape in Sri Lanka); "Human Rights: The Bedroom Has Gone Global," *Inter Press Service*, September 14, 1995 (Austria criminalized marital rape in 1989); "Sex &

Love & Morality = Confusion; Chinese Women Finding Line Between 'Right' and 'Wrong' Has Blurred," *Washington Post*, August 23, 1995, p. A28 (reporting on "what is believed to have been the first case concerning marital rape in China"). See also Department of State, *Country Reports on Human Rights Practices* (1994): 1256 (Comm. Print 1995) (marital rape is not a crime in Pakistan); "Marital Rape Kept Out of UN Resolution," *Chicago Tribune*, May 8, 1995, p. 3 (reporting that Muslim delegates to a United Nations crime prevention conference deleted all references to marital rape in the conference resolution on extradition, arguing that marital rape is not a crime in many countries); "Saying 'No' to HIV Sex Partner," *New Straits Times Press*, December 18, 1995, p. 20 (Malaysian government has no plans to criminalize marital rape); "Family Violence Bill Will Give More Power to Police Courts," *The Straits Times Press*, September 28, 1995, p. 24 (a new statute is introduced in Singapore that if passed would criminalize marital rape).

37. If Jaggar had considered that a major alternative to liberal individualism, in world-metaphysical terms, is the Buddhist denial of the self, would she have spoken so slightingly of individualism?

38. J. S. Mill, *The Subjection of Women*, ed. S. M. Okin (Indianapolis: Hackett, 1988), p. 33.

39. His reference to *Uncle Tom's Cabin* in this passage makes it clear that he is thinking about America, and yet he appears to be ignorant of the sexual situation of American slaves.

40. Ibid., pp. 33–34. Mill here discusses the Infant Custody Act of 1839, which allowed the Court of Chancery to award mothers custody of children under the age of seven and access to those under the age of sixteen; this small beginning shows graphically how bad the legal situation of mothers was previously.

41. Ibid., pp. 86–88. Compare *Considerations on Representative Government*, where Mill observes that a man who takes no pleasure in his wife's pleasure is "stunted."

42. Ibid., p. 86.

43. See *A Theory of Justice*, pp. 128 f. The focus here is on intergenerational justice, and the issue of distribution to the current members of the household is not raised. On p. 463, Rawls states that in a "broader inquiry" the institution of the family "might be questioned, and other arrangements might indeed prove to be preferable."

44. Gary Becker, *A Treatise on the Family* (Cambridge: Harvard University Press, 1981). In his 1992 Nobel Prize address, "The Economic Way of Looking at Behavior," now reprinted in *The Essence of Becker* (Stanford, Calif.: Hoover Press, 1995), pp. 633–654, Becker states that his model assumed too much altruism. "Many economists, including me, have excessively relied on altruism to tie together the interests of family members" (p. 648). Becker here remarks that we should not return to a narrow focus on self-interest, but should recognize that a whole host of attitudes, including obligation, anger, and others—attitudes that will vary among individuals in accordance with their early experiences—influence the behavior of family members toward one another.

45. See Susan Moller Okin, *Women in Western Political Thought* (Princeton: Princeton University Press, 1979), p. 282, on the way in which Mill's proposals showed the limitations of previous liberal individualism.

46. See Amartya Sen, "Gender and Cooperative Conflicts," in *Persistent Inequalities,* ed. I. Tinker (New York: Oxford University Press, 1990), pp. 123–149.

47. For one impressive critique of the U.S. tax system's inequities toward women, and a proposal for reform, see Edward McCaffery, *Taxing Women* (Chicago: University of Chicago Press, 1996). McCaffery is a political liberal in the Rawlsian tradition; see, for example, his "The Political Liberal Case Against the Estate Tax," *Philosophy and Public Affairs* 23 (1994):281–312.

48. See Verma, "Femininity, Equality, and Personhood," p. 441.

49. Rawls, *Theory of Justice,* p. 7.

50. Okin, *Women in Western Political Thought,* p. 97. She does not, however, address the issue that is really central to Rawls in the context, namely, the question whether the parties would represent continuing transgenerational lines or simply themselves. See Rawls, *A Theory of Justice,* pp. 146, 284 ff.

51. S. M. Okin, *Justice, Gender, and the Family* (New York: Basic Books, 1989). The proposal to make the basic structure of society nongendered does not, of course, imply that gender might not continue to play a role in the private lives of individuals, much as ethnicity or culture could play a role. Among concrete issues, Okin is particularly concerned with the situation of women in the event of divorce; she urges that women who have done housework to facilitate a spouse's career development be entitled to a substantial share of his income.

52. J. Rawls, "Feminist Critique of Liberalism," draft. Rawls says that it was always his intention that the parties in the original position do not know the sex of those they represent; he points to p. 99, where he says that distinctions of sex are like distinctions of race and culture: they are based on "fixed natural characteristics" and they often influence people's life chances from the very start. It should be clear, he says, that the Veil of Ignorance is designed to ensure the parties' ignorance of all features that have this character. Sex (unlike gender, which is a social and institutional category) is a place in the distribution of natural endowments and abilities. (See also "Fairness to Goodness," *Philosophical Review* 84 [1975]:536–554, esp. p. 537, where Rawls states that the parties do not know their sex.) He also states in *A Theory of Justice,* and reaffirms in the unpublished draft, that the family is certainly a part of the basic structure of society, to be constrained by the principles of justice. These will ensure that women who for religious or other reasons, wish to choose a traditional role are free to do so; nonetheless, political principles impose constraints on the family as an institution to guarantee the basic rights, liberties, and fair opportunities of all its members. There may be a difference between Rawls and Okin, in that Okin would seem to insist that the internal workings of the family should be governed by principles of justice, whereas Rawls envisages the principles of justice operating as constraints on what families may choose, but not as governing its internal workings. The extent to which this is a serious difference needs further examination. The draft has never been published, so these remarks should not be regarded as definitive or final. Rawls continues to work on this topic, and a revised and expanded version of his view appears in J. Rawls, "The Idea of Public Reason," *University of Chicago Law Review* 64 (1997):765–807.

53. C. Bunch, "Women's Rights as Human Rights: Toward a Re-Vision of Human Rights," *Human Rights Quarterly* 12 (1990):486–498; see also Bunch, "Trans-

forming Human Rights from a Feminist Perspective," in *Women's Rights, Human Rights*, pp. 11–17; and Elisabeth Friedman, "Women's Human Rights: The Emergence of a Movement," in *Women's Rights, Human Rights*, pp. 18–35.

54. Described in Sara Hossain, "Women's Rights and Personal Laws in South Asia," in *Human Rights of Women: National and International Perspectives*, ed. Rebecca Cook (Philadelphia: University of Pennsylvania Press, 1994), pp. 465–494.

55. *Nelly Zaman v. Ghiyasuddin*, 34 D.L.R. 221 (1982). This case is discussed in Martha Nussbaum, "Religion and Women's Human Rights," in *Religion and Contemporary Liberalism*, ed. Paul Weitham (Notre Dame, Ind.: University of Notre Dame Press, 1997), pp. 93–137. In revised form this article forms chapter 3 of Martha Nussbaum, *Sex and Social Justice* (New York: Oxford University Press, in press).

56. See Martha Chen, *A Quiet Revolution: Women in Transition in Rural Bangladesh* (Cambridge, Mass.: Schenkman, 1983).

57. Mill notes that when an opinion is grounded in reason, a good counterargument will shake its solidity; when it is grounded in irrational desires and fears, good counterarguments merely intensify the resistance: "The worse it fares in argumentative contest, the more persuaded its adherents are that their feeling must have some deeper ground, which the arguments do not reach; and while the feeling remains, it is always throwing up fresh entrenchments of argument to repair any breach made in the old" (*Subjection of Women*, pp. 1–2).

58. See MacKinnon, *Toward a Feminist Theory of the State* (Cambridge: Harvard University Press, 1989), pp. 40 ff.; "Reflections on Sex Equality Under Law," *Yale Law Journal* 100 (1991):1281–1328; Jaggar, *Feminist Politics*, pp. 181 ff. (noting that liberal feminists have been gradually led to abandon the excessively formal approach).

59. "Toward Neutral Principles of Constitutional Law," *Harvard Law Review* 73 (1959):1–35. I discuss Wechsler's argument in detail in *Poetic Justice: The Literary Imagination and Public Life* (Boston: Beacon, 1996), chap. 4.

60. See my *Poetic Justice*, chap. 4.

61. To some extent, these criticisms are probably inspired by the similar criticism of liberalism made by Marx, for example in *Critique of the Gotha Program*, where Marx argues that the liberal idea of "equal rights" is "constantly stigmatized by a bourgeois limitation," namely, the neglect of the antecedent role of differences of class and wealth in affecting the productivity of individuals. "It is, therefore, a right of inequality, in its content, like every right. ... To avoid all these defects, right instead of being equal would have to be unequal." MacKinnon's critique in *Toward a Feminist Theory of the State* is explicitly inspired by the Marxian critique.

62. See Gary Becker and Guity Nashat Becker, *The Economics of Life: From Baseball to Affirmative Action to Immigration, How Real-World Issues Affect Our Everyday Life* (New York: McGraw-Hill, 1997), pp. 287–288.

63. This is not to deny that individual liberal thinkers have made such commitments; and here the libertarian tradition could justly be suspected of having departed from the main line of the liberal tradition, with its strong emphasis on the critique of hierarchies and of the social ascendancy of morally irrelevant distinctions.

64. For this view in a feminist context, see Sen, "Gender Inequality and Theories of Justice," and Nussbaum, "Human Capabilities, Female Human Beings," both in *Women, Culture, and Development*, pp. 259–573, 61–104.

65. See also Joseph Raz, *The Morality of Freedom* (Oxford: Clarendon Press, 1986).

66. This is brought out by Sen in "Freedoms and Needs," *The New Republic*, January 10/17, 1994, and by me in "The Good as Discipline, the Good as Freedom," in *The Ethics of Consumption and Global Stewardship*, ed. David Crocker and Tony Linden (Totowa, N.J.: Rowman and Littlefield, 1997), pp. 312–341.

67. See *A Theory of Justice*, pp. 201–228, on the equal worth of liberty, and pp. 73, 83–89, on fair equality of opportunity.

68. Not all—see Christina Hoff Sommers, *Who Stole Feminism? How Women Have Betrayed Women* (New York: Simon and Schuster, 1994), discussing the history of "equity feminism" in the suffrage movement.

69. For the roles that the imagination should play in developing a liberal theory of the public sphere, see my *Poetic Justice*.

70. See the discussion of this second criticism in Onora O'Neill, "Justice, Gender, and International Boundaries," in *The Quality of Life*, ed. M. Nussbaum and A. Sen (Oxford: Clarendon Press, 1993), pp. 279–323. The feminists criticized by O'Neill include Carol Gilligan, Eva Kittay, Genevieve Lloyd, Sara Ruddick, and Nel Noddings.

71. This point was well made by Marx in *On the Jewish Question*, where—responding to Bauer's contention that a person could not qua Jew acquire "the rights of man"—he replies that "the incompatibility between religion and the rights of man is so little manifest in the concept of the rights of man that the *right to be religious*, in one's own fashion, and to practise one's own particular religion, is expressly included among the rights of man. The privilege of faith is a *universal right of man*." Unfortunately, Marx (apparently neglecting this insight) goes on to claim that the "rights of man" treat the individual as purely self-centered, "separated from the community, withdrawn into himself, wholly preoccupied with his private interest and acting in accordance with his private caprice." This mistaken claim has probably influenced some feminist critiques.

72. Or, in the case of Rawls, to talents and propensities not integrally bound up with basic rational humanity.

73. See, for example, Rawls, *A Theory of Justice*, p. 207: "to gamble in this way [by allowing the public realm to restrict the liberty of conscience] would show that one did not take one's religious or moral convictions seriously, or highly value the liberty to examine one's beliefs."

74. For a mordant account of those traditions in their relation to feminism, see Verma, "Femininity, Equality, and Personhood."

75. Maistre ridiculed liberalism by saying that "there is no such thing as *man* in the world. I have seen, during my life, Frenchmen, Italians, Russians, etc. . . . But as far as *man* is concerned, I declare that I have never in my life met him; if he exists, he is unknown to me" (cited in Stephen Holmes, *The Anatomy of Antiliberalism* [Cambridge: Harvard University Press, 1993], p. 14). Notice, however, that Maistre is perfectly happy to use high-level abstractions such as "Frenchman," which is, one could argue, far less likely than is "human being" to reveal a set of

common features similar across all cases. Compare MacKinnon, "From Practice to Theory, or What Is a White Woman Anyway?" *Yale Journal of Law and Feminism* 4 (1991):13–22, who criticizes antiessentialist feminists for using race and class as legitimate categories while refusing the same legitimacy to gender.

76. See Friedman in "Feminism and Modern Friendship."

77. MacKinnon's own degree of "essentialism" about the situation of women has come under sharp attack from communitarian and postmodernist feminists; see the discussion in Elizabeth Rappaport, "Generalizing Gender: Reason and Essence in the Legal Thought of Catharine MacKinnon," in *A Mind of One's Own: Feminist Essays on Reason and Objectivity*, ed. L. Antony and C. Witt (Boulder, Colo.: Westview, 1993), pp. 127–144, strongly supporting MacKinnon's essentialism; and see MacKinnon, "From Practice to Theory, or What Is a White Woman Anyway?" criticizing Elizabeth Spelman's *Inessential Woman* (London: Women's Press, 1990). In her article "Feminist Metaphysics," in *A Mind of One's Own*, pp. 273–288, Charlotte Witt argues, plausibly, that MacKinnon needs, and relies on, an idea of the human being, not just an idea of woman. For an excellent discussion of the entire topic, see Charlotte Witt, "Anti-Essentialism in Feminist Theory," *Philosophical Topics* 23 (1995): 321–344.

78. Onora O'Neill, "Justice, Gender, and International Boundaries." The article constructs an illuminating parallel between the gender boundary and cultural/national boundaries. On gender "essentialism," see also C. MacKinnon, "From Practice to Theory, or What Is a White Woman Anyway?"; and Susan Moller Okin, "Inequalities Between the Sexes in Different Cultural Contexts," in *Women, Culture, and Development*, pp. 274–297.

79. See also Nussbaum, "Human Capabilities, Female Human Beings," in *Women, Culture, and Development*, pp. 360–395.

80. Jaggar, *Feminist Politics*, p. 28.

81. On Astell, see Margaret Atherton, "Cartesian Reason and Gendered Reason," in *A Mind of One's Own*, pp. 19–34. Astell's major works are now reprinted in *Astell: Political Writing*, ed. Mary Springborg (Cambridge: Cambridge University Press, 1996). On Musonius, see Cora Lutz, "Musonius Rufus: 'The Roman Socrates,'" *Yale Classical Studies* (1947): 1–147; Nussbaum, "The Incomplete Feminism of Musonius Rufus," in Nussbaum, *Sex and Social Justice*; and Nussbaum, *The Therapy of Desire: Theory and Practice in Hellenistic Ethics* (Princeton: Princeton University Press, 1994), chap. 9; on Greek Stoic attitudes to the equality of women, see Malcolm Schofield, *The Stoic Idea of the City* (Cambridge: Cambridge University Press, 1991).

82. Noam Chomsky, *Cartesian Linguistics: A Chapter in the History of Rationalist Thought* (New York: Harper and Row, 1966).

83. See Nussbaum, "Emotions and Women's Capabilities," in *Women, Culture, and Development*; also Anne Fausto-Sterling, *Myths of Gender*, 2d ed. (New York: Basic Books, 1992).

84. Some examples include Carol Gilligan, *In a Different Voice* (Cambridge: Harvard University Press, 1982); Nancy Chodorow, *The Reproduction of Mothering* (Berkeley: University of California Press, 1978); Virginia Held, *Feminist Morality: Transforming Culture, Society, and Politics* (Chicago: University of Chicago Press, 1993).

85. For criticisms of the reason-emotion contrast, see Martha Minow and Elizabeth Spelman, "Passions Within Reason," *Cardozo Law Review* 10 (1988):37–76; M. Nussbaum, *Poetic Justice*.

86. See, for example, Catherine Lutz, *Unnatural Emotions: Everyday Sentiments on a Micronesian Atoll and Their Challenge to Western Theory* (Chicago: University of Chicago Press, 1988); Helen Longino, "To See Feelingly: Reason, Passion, and Dialogue," in *Feminisms in the Academy*, ed. D. Stanton and A. Stewart (Ann Arbor: University of Michigan Press, 1995), pp. 19–45.

87. This is the theme of my Gifford lectures at the University of Edinburgh, 1993, published as *Upheavals of Thought: A Theory of the Emotions* (Cambridge: Cambridge University Press, 1993). See also D. Kahan and M. Nussbaum, "Two Conceptions of Emotions in Criminal Law," *Columbia Law Review* 96 (1996): 270–374.

88. See Genevieve Lloyd, *The Man of Reason*, 2d ed. (London: Routledge, 1993); Lutz, *Unnatural Emotions*.

89. Annette Baier, "Hume: The Reflective Woman's Epistemologist," in *A Mind of One's Own*.

90. For a trenchant critique that has not been displaced, see Anthony Kenny, in *Action, Emotion, and Will* (London: Routledge and Kegan Paul, 1963), pp. 1 ff.

91. See Longino, "To See Feelingly," summarizing the positions of Lloyd and others. A prominent source of this position within feminism is the psychoanalytical work of Nancy Chodorow in *The Reproduction of Mothering*.

92. Nel Noddings, *Caring: A Feminine Approach to Ethics and Moral Education* (Berkeley: University of California Press, 1984). I do not discuss the even more influential views of Carol Gilligan, since it is very unclear what Gilligan's normative view is, and also what analysis she gives to emotions of love and care (to what extent she connects them with thought).

93. Noddings's general position is that the notions of "justification, fairness, justice" are "the language of the father" and that the primary defect in contemporary ethical thought is that it focuses on this voice rather than on the "mother's voice" (p. 1, et passim).

94. A fruitful comparison would be to the more extensive assault on liberal reciprocity in the work of Emmanuel Levinas. Noddings herself does not discuss Levinas, but she does connect her idea to Martin Buber's account of the I-Thou relation (*Caring*, p. 142).

95. Noddings, *Caring*, p. 137. This forms part of Noddings's argument against Sartre's claim that emotion always has an intentional object.

96. Perhaps I am handicapped by the fact that I simply do not recognize my own experience of motherhood in Noddings's descriptions of fusing and bonding. My first sharp impression of Rachel Nussbaum was as a pair of feet drumming on my diaphragm with a certain distinct separateness, a pair of arms flexing their muscles against my bladder. Before even her hair got into the world a separate voice could be heard inside, proclaiming its individuality or even individualism, and it has not stopped arguing yet, twenty-three years later. I am sure RN would be quite outraged by the suggestion that her own well-being was at any time merged with that of her mother, and her mother would never dare to make such an overweening suggestion. This liberal experience of maternity as

the give and take of argument has equipped me ill to understand the larger mysteries of Noddings's text.

97. See the acute criticism of Noddings in Diana Fritz Cates, *Choosing to Feel: Virtue, Friendship, and Compassion for Friends* (Notre Dame, Ind.: Notre Dame University Press, 1996).

98. Nietzsche, *Thus Spoke Zarathustra*, trans. W. A. Kauffman (Harmondsworth, U.K.: Penguin, 1978), pt. 1, "On the Teachers of Virtue." (Kaufmann translates *einnicken* as "drop off," but I have substituted a more literal rendering.)

99. This is Bernard Williams's phrase ("Persons, Character, and Morality," in *Moral Luck: Philosophical Papers 1973–80* [Cambridge: Cambridge University Press 1981], p. 18), used in criticism of impartialist views of responsibility that would urge us to reflect on whether we may or may not give special privileges to our own family. Williams says that if a man on a raft, knowing that he can save either his wife or a stranger, but not both, pauses to deliberate at all, he is having "one thought too many." I am not making any claim here about that particular case, but it seems likely that a communitarian might say something similar about cases of female self-sacrifice for family, and there I would wish to insist on the relevance of reason, given the social deformation of the norms in question.

100. V. Das and R. Nicholas, "'Welfare' and 'Well-Being' in South Asian Societies," ACLS-SSRC Joint Committee on South Asia (New York: Social Science Research Council, 1981).

101. See also Marcia Homiak, "Feminism and Aristotle's Rational Ideal," in *A Mind of One's Own*, pp. 1–17; Jean Hampton, "Feminist Contractarianism," in *A Mind of One's Own*, pp. 227–255; Susan Okin, "Reason and Feeling in Thinking About Justice," *Ethics* 99 (1989): 229–249.

102. See MacKinnon, *Feminism Unmodified* (Cambridge: Harvard University Press, 1987); Andrea Dworkin, *Intercourse* (New York: Free Press, 1988).

103. See Amartya Sen, "Gender Inequality and Theories of Justice," and also his "Gender and Cooperative Conflicts"; J. Elster, *Sour Grapes* (Cambridge: Cambridge University Press, 1983); John C. Harsanyi, "Morality and the Theory of Rational Behavior," in *Utilitarianism and Beyond*, ed. A. Sen and B. Williams (Cambridge: Cambridge University Press, 1982), pp. 39–62.

104. Jean-Jacques Rousseau, *Émile*, bk. 4.

105. Adam Smith, *The Theory of Moral Sentiments* (Oxford: Clarendon Press, 1976), pts. 1, 3. The remarks especially critical of greed and competition are primarily from the later editions. On Smith's changing attitudes to acquisitiveness, see Ian Simpson Ross, *The Life of Adam Smith* (Oxford: Clarendon Press, 1995).

106. This is clearer in the case of Rousseau than in that of Smith; see Joshua Cohen, "The Natural Goodness of Humanity," in *Reclaiming the History of Ethics: Essays for John Rawls,* ed. Andrew Reath, Barbara Herman, and Christine Korsgaard (Cambridge: Cambridge University Press, 1997), pp. 102–149. Smith is even more profoundly influenced by Stoicism than is Rousseau, and the primary emphasis in his critique of desire and emotion is placed on distorting social forces.

107. Mill, *Subjection of Women*, pp. 22–23; the judgment of naturalness is said by Mill to be made "with that inability to recognise their own work which distinguishes the unanalytic mind"; see also p. 12: "Was there ever any domination which did not appear natural to those who possessed it?" and p. 84: "How rarely

it is that even men complain of the general order of society; and how much rarer still would such complaint be, if they did not know of any different order existing anywhere else."

108. Mill, *Subjection of Women*, p. 16.

109. Ibid.

110. Ibid., pp. 12–13.

111. Both Rousseau and Smith, for example, seem to hold this, although Rousseau's argument about the naturalness of gender distinctions is notoriously difficult to interpret. See S. M. Okin, *Women in Western Political Thought* (Princeton: Princeton University Press, 1979).

112. See my "Objectification," *Philosophy and Public Affairs,* Fall 1995, pp. 249–291; Barbara Herman, "Could It Be Worth Thinking with Kant About Sex and Marriage?" in *A Mind of One's Own.*

113. See my argument in "Objectification."

114. Mill, *Subjection of Women*, p. 53.

115. Catharine MacKinnon, *Feminism Unmodified*, p. 45.

116. See my "Feminists and Philosophy," *New York Review of Books*, October 20, 1994.

117. Kant, conclusion to *Critique of Practical Reason*. The origin of this passage is probably found in Seneca, *Moral Epistle* 40; see my "Kant and Stoic Cosmopolitanism" in the *Journal of Political Philosophy*, forthcoming.

2

Women's Rights: Whose Obligations?

Onora O'Neill

A Martian or a Venusian, listening to the public rhetoric of our day—the ordinary pronouncements of politicians and the ordinary reports of the media—might conclude that we take rights very seriously indeed, even that we are obsessed by them. She might even conclude that we take the rights of women very seriously indeed. Women's rights may have seemed shocking when Mary Wollstonecraft chose the title of *A Vindication of the Rights of Woman* in 1790; now they are part of the rhetoric both of the established order and of its critics. They elicit more yawns and inattention than hostility, although there is still a bit of that.

Taking the rhetoric seriously is one thing; taking the substance seriously another. One of the main uses of this rhetoric is to point out how often human rights, and with them women's rights, are violated. No doubt a gap between rhetoric and reality is unsurprising; but this gap is more than evidence of failure to practice what we preach. Putting the matter starkly, if we think about justice primarily in terms of rights we are more or less bound to find not only that we do not or cannot live up to it, but that we cannot work out what we are trying to live up to. The rhetoric of rights is not only deceptively easy to promulgate, but deeply evasive. Most of the difficulty of thinking about women's rights grows out of this general evasiveness of thought about rights, so it is to this pervasive difficulty rather than to battles about the rights women should have that I shall turn first.

Rights and Obligations

In speaking of the rhetoric of rights as evasive I do not mean to suggest that human rights, or women's rights, are unimportant, or that securing them is an unimportant political goal. My concern is rather that talking as if rights were the core of justice, and rights for women the core of justice for women, is a lazy way of talking and of thinking, which systematically obscures what we would most need to think about and to do if we were to take rights seriously.

We often talk of having rights. This gives rights a nice substantial feel, as though they were bits of hardware that could be touched and traded, purloined or protected. This way of talking misleads. Talking of rights and of obligations are both ways of talking about action, not about items that can be possessed. Moreover, most important rights are intrinsically relational in that they are claim rights, which mirror certain sorts of obligation: both claim rights and the corresponding obligations are a matter of required types of action, or of omission.[1] When we talk of such rights we look at the required action from the perspective of the claimant or right-holder; when we talk of obligations we look at required action from the perspective of the obligation-bearer, of the one who is to act. So it is clear enough that there will be no claim rights unless others have obligations. If anyone is to have a right of free association, then everyone must have an obligation not to obstruct free association. If anyone is to have a right to information about family planning, then someone, or perhaps a number of people, must have an obligation to make that information available. If anyone is to have a right of access to children with whom they do not live, others must have obligations to allow that access and to ensure that it is not thwarted. If anyone is to have a right to a free or even to an affordable nursery place for her pre-school children then somebody, and probably many people, must have obligations to contribute to providing that nursery place.

So far, so commonplace. In a way the fact that there are no claim rights without obligations is so obvious and well-known that it is embarrassing to bring the matter up. Yet I believe that a great deal of discussion of rights, including of women's rights, continually misstates the ways in which and the extent to which rights and obligations correspond to one another, and hence fails to see how much it matters whether discussion of justice emphasizes rights or obligations.

There are two very general reasons why starting with rights is a lop-sided way of thinking about ethics, and even about justice. The first and the more general, to which I shall return, is that while claim rights are mirror images of obligations, not all obligations have mirror images. If there are obligations without corresponding rights it will evidently impoverish moral thinking if one starts with the rights and leaves aside those obligations not mirrored by any rights. This thought by itself is reason enough to begin with obligations and not with rights. To do otherwise is about as sensible as trying to count the adult population of a country by counting all the parents, so overlooking all childless persons. However, for the moment I shall leave aside this large reason for starting with the obligations rather than the rights, and consider why the rhetoric of rights has such great capacities to dash the very hopes of justice that it raises.

The second very general reason why the rhetoric of rights creates problems is not that it is blind to obligations without counterpart rights, but that it obscures what is really at stake by focussing on the rights rather than the obligations. The obscurity arises because claim rights are easy to proclaim without paying much attention to the obligations which are their counterparts. This deceptive convenience is due, at least in large measure, to the fact that it is so easy to slide between discussion of positive (institutional, customary) rights and of moral (natural, human) rights. Everybody acknowledges that positive claim rights must have well-defined corresponding obligations: to speak of them as positive is just to speak of them as institutionalised, and we are evidently speaking of one and the same set of institutionalized requirements for action (or forbearance) when we speak of positive claim rights and of their corresponding obligations. However, the point of appealing to human rights, or to women's rights, is not to endorse the positive rights embedded in existing institutions. The point is often to challenge existing positive rights (or their absence) and, of course, existing positive obligations (or their absence), or to justify different rights and different corollary obligations. What would be the point of appealing to human rights if they were no more than the institutionalised rights of some social order, or the various vestigially institutionalized 'manifesto rights' promulgated in Charters and Declarations, however august? The rhetoric of rights supposedly appeals to fundamental moral principles, and aspires to justify or to condemn institutional and positive rights, and indeed to justify or to condemn the claims of the grand Declarations and Charters, so cannot coherently presuppose them.

But once we start talking about moral (human, natural) rights, and however we think they are to be justified, it becomes easy to let questions about obligations drift out of sight. The Rights of Man have much more immediate charm than the Duties of Man; and equally the Rights of Women can have much more immediate charm than the Duties of Women—let alone than the duties that correspond to the Rights of Women.

It is easy to succumb to the charm of rights, and delightful to think about claiming them. Claiming that one has a right, whether to certain liberties or to security, or to goods or services, perhaps to welfare, can be heady stuff. It is a matter of thinking about what one ought to get or to have done for one, and about what others (but which others?) ought to do or provide for one. Of course, claims are not likely to be effective unless somebody ought to meet those claims, and often they will be ineffective unless the claims are not merely allocated to some agent or agency, but accepted and enforceable. But the actual claiming can go on loudly and confidently, with panache and bravado, without establishing who should deliver whatever is claimed. It is even possible to claim what nobody can deliver as a right: I was once publicly admonished for asking who holds the obligations that correspond to an alleged right to health (not merely to a right to health-care) on the grounds that health is too important to human beings not to be the object of a right.

Moreover, there can be political and rhetorical advantage as well as charm in being vague about obligations. Claims about rights need only assert what right-holders are entitled to; only the curmudgeonly will object. Others may be animated and have their hopes raised. But claims about obligations have to specify not only what is to be accorded, but which obligation-bearers are going to have to do what for whom and at what cost. This is a much less charming thought. Unsurprisingly the rhetoric of obligations and duties has an unsavoury reputation, and those on whom burdens may fall often object.

Yet strangely the rhetoric of rights is often praised for taking human agents and their dignity seriously. When we think of others as right-holders it is, of course, true that we no longer think of them as mere subjects, who plead abjectly for better treatment. We think of right-holders as full persons, as citizens or citizens-to-be. Yet when claimants point to others' (but which others'?) duties they do not have to take much action, and may even wrap themselves passively in a cloak of grievance or of resentment. They do not need to work out who will have to do what for whom at what cost, let alone what they themselves will have to do at what costs to themselves. In short, the rhetoric of rights, although more active than a rhetoric of dependent pleading, of mere subjects, is still a rhetoric of recipience rather than of activism. It still takes the perspective of the claimant rather than of the contributor, of the consumer rather than the producer, of the passive rather than of the active citizen.

Liberty and Welfare

Of course, these points are hardly novel. They have surfaced repeatedly in the truly enormous contemporary literature on theories of justice. Much of this literature argues for rights and assumes that if claim rights can be established, then obligations will follow calmly in their wake. This theoretical literature may lack the full charm and bravado, let alone the political bite, of more public uses of the rhetoric of rights, but much of it shares the intellectual failings of claims to rights, in that it takes obligations less seriously than rights.

These failings crop up repeatedly in the prolific disputes about justice during the last twenty-five years. The most enduring of these disputes has been between more and less libertarian thinkers and advocates of various conceptions of social justice. Libertarians have argued that all universal claim rights are liberty rights with corollary obligations not to interfere. The advocates of social justice have argued that there are also universal claim rights to certain goods or services, and in particular to welfare, with corollary obligations to deliver the goods.

All advocates of rights are agreed that *if* there are universal claim rights to liberty, then the corollary obligations must also be universal. For example, a right not to be raped, or a right to compete with others for employment, will be marred if it is a right against some but not against all others. If there were some others who have no obligation to refrain from raping, or no obligation to let others compete in the market place, then nobody would have an unrestricted right to either. Mere liberties apart, universal liberty rights require corresponding universal obligations.

Libertarian advocates of rights insist also that universal claim rights *must* be liberty rights, and that universal rights to goods or services, hence to welfare, are incoherent. Goods and services have to be delivered at particular times and places, hence by particular agents and agencies. They cannot be delivered by everybody rushing in everywhere and treading on one another's toes. There can be no universal obligations to provide goods and services that correspond to universal rights to goods and services *in the same way that universal obligations to respect others' liberties correspond to universal liberty rights*. It follows, they conclude, that there cannot be universal rights to goods and services, hence that there can be no universal economic, social or cultural rights, and that the august Charters and Declarations make incoherent claims, which can indeed be put to rhetorical use, but can only disappoint those who take them seriously.

This libertarian line of thought is often extended with the claim that since there can be no universal rights to goods and services, any such rights must be not universal but "special" rights, to which the "special" obligations of specified parties correspond. In short, rights to goods and services and obligations to provide them are inevitably not moral or human rights at all. They are only the institutionalised or positive rights of a specific social order or reflections of a specific contractual arrangement or social role.

The implications of this line of thought can bite hard. For example, libertarians will agree that the staff of a maternity ward may have an obligation of care—a special obligation—to those patients who have been appropriately admitted, and those patients may have a special right to care from that staff. But they will deny that the staff have any more general obligations to provide care, or pregnant women a more general right to claim care. This line of thought accepts that all rights to goods and services are special rights, that presuppose the specific relationships that may be established, for example, by legislation or by contract, by custom or by practice. Which sorts of special rights to goods or services and which sorts of special obligations are to be established is left entirely open. Special obligations to provide and rights to receive medical care and attention from the staff of a maternity ward may be on a footing with special obligations to shackle women prisoners even when in labour and special rights to be protected from the threat of women in labour absconding.[2] On this account, rights to goods and services are not human or moral rights at all; they are no more than instances of the very sorts of institutional rights which the rhetoric of rights aspires to criticise.

But the argument is not sound. All that follows from the convincing thought that universal rights to goods and services cannot be matched by universally delivered obligations to provide at all relevant times and places is that *if* there are universal rights to goods and services, then aspects of the corresponding obligations which have to do with delivery will have to take a different form. There is no intrinsic problem here. While it is true that a right not to be raped, or a right to compete for employment, is marred unless the counterpart obligation is universally held, this is not true of rights to goods and services. If, for example, persons with dependent children have a right to adequate housing, then the right can be fully met if *somebody*—or *some body*—provides each such person who lacks housing with adequate housing. It is not necessary that everyone contribute to provision, and wholly counter-productive, not to say impossible, if everyone attempts to be the provider on all occasions. Or if women have a right to ante-natal medical care, then it will be enough if *some* medically qualified persons provide that care to each woman—and downright dangerous, not to mention exhausting, and ultimately impossible, if everybody medically qualified tries to do so for each or all women.

In short the obligations that correspond to rights to goods and services *must* differ in form from at least some of the obligations that correspond to liberty rights. Universal rights to goods and services are quite coherent,[3] provided that some aspects of the counterpart obligations which have to do with delivery are *distributed* or *allocated* to specific agents and agencies. However, those aspects of the counterpart obligations which have to do with *determining a scheme of delivery*, or with *refraining from obstructing delivery*, or with *contributing proportionally to costs* can quite well be universally held obligations. Hence rights to goods and services can be equated neither with special rights nor with liberty rights.

Evidently, a universal right to some good or service is not taken seriously unless specific obligations to deliver the relevant good or service are established, so ensuring that the right is secured for each, so for all right-holders. We are quite familiar with the thought that universal rights can be met distributively, and can point to many cases where universal welfare rights have been established within the domain of certain states by distributing obligations to provide welfare to cover each, hence all, right holders. Those who established such welfare rights did not miraculously work out how everybody within those states could be omnipresent, forever fulfilling obligations to deliver food or medical care or housing to each and so to all, or even to all in need. What they did was hard enough, but it wasn't physically impossible.

There are then, as libertarians insist, certain clear disanalogies between universal liberty rights and certain otherwise amorphous universal rights to goods and services. However, the libertarian claim that universal rights to goods and services are incoherent has not been established. The disanalogy might be summarised as follows: the conclusion of libertarian arguments is a *political agenda*: a particular list of liberty rights and their corresponding universal obligations is to be secured. The conclusion of a social justice line of thought combines parts of the libertarian agenda—a rather more restricted set of liberty rights is to be secured—with an open *political debate* rather than with a further list of rights: certain universal rights to goods and services are to be secured by establishing one of many possible schemes which distribute obligations to deliver those rights for each and so for all.

Some social justice liberals have queried this disanalogy.[4] They suggest that there are no serious differences between universal liberty rights and universal rights to goods and services. They point out, for example, that even impeccable liberty rights with well defined counterpart obligations—a right not to be tortured, a right not to be raped—cannot be secured without complex institutions which will adjudicate cases and enforce rights. Liberty rights and their corresponding obligations may need police, courts, and many other forms of accountability if they are to be enforced; institutions of enforcement too have to distribute obligations for specific aspects of enforcement according to one or another scheme. So liberty rights too are amorphous until one or another institutional scheme has been established, which determines who bears the counterpart obligations.

However, there are deeper discrepancies between liberty rights and rights to goods and services than this attempt to yoke them allows. To be sure, the *enforcement* of liberty rights, or rather of their corresponding obligations, needs institutions: hardly news. However, the correspondence of universal liberty rights to universal obligations is relatively well-defined even when institutions are missing or weak. For example, a violation of a right not to be raped or of a right not to be tortured may be clear enough, and the perpetrator may even be identifiable, even when institutions for enforcement are lamentably weak. But the correspondence of universal rights to goods and services to obligations to *provide* or *deliver* remains far more amorphous when institutions are missing or weak. Somebody who receives no maternity care may no doubt *claim* that her rights have been violated, but unless obligations to deliver that care have been established and distributed, she will not know where to press her claim, and it will be systematically obscure whether there is any perpetrator, or who has neglected or violated her rights.

Rights to goods and services can be thought of only in the hazy, amorphous way which the rhetoric of rights favours and allows until they are at least partly institutionalized. It may be possible to state *what* ought to be provided or delivered, but it will be impossible to state *who* ought to do the providing or delivering, and *who* can be called to account when deliveries are botched, or nothing is delivered, unless there are established institutions and well defined special relationships. Rights to goods and services are easy to proclaim, but until there are effective institutions their proclamation may seem bitter mockery to those who most need them. Liberty rights, however, are different because far more is determined even when institutions are missing or weak: as soon as it is possible to state what ought to be provided—non-interference—it will also be possible to state who ought to provide: everyone and all institutions ought to do so. Institutions come into the picture subsequently for purposes of enforcement. By contrast, when we discuss obligations, of whatever sort, we immediately have to consider *whose* obligations we have in mind and so will define *against whom* rights holders may lodge their claims.

Women's Rights

How does this matter for women, and for women's rights? A small, and once again embarrassingly commonplace, reminder may be helpful here. In speaking of women's rights most people have meant to speak of rights that men have, which women should have as well. They have not generally meant to speak of any distinctive rights which women should have and men should not. The exception—not without controversy or importance—lies in rights that are quite specifically connected to differences of sex and reproduction. Rights to maternity services would properly be women's rights and not men's. But men too may have rights not be raped, as women too may have rights to vote and rights of association.

However, it is evident that the sorts of rights to goods and services on which women and men may rely most frequently can often differ. For example, as long as women still carry more of the real work of caring for true dependents (children, those who are ill, the elderly) and as long as they have fewer resources with which to do so, they will need rights to financial support and to relevant social services more often. Equally, as long as a disproportionate amount of juvenile crime is committed by boys and young men, their need for rights of due process and for other relevant social services will be greater than that of girls and women of like age. However, such differences in (average) situation do not show that women's rights should differ from men's rights outside the areas of maternity care and the like. It is not surprising that for most of its history the women's movement has been a movement that claimed for women the same rights as were claimed for men—from rights to hold property, to the franchise, to rights to enter all lines of employment.

Only since the 1970s have parts of the women's movement taken quite another turn. Some recent and influential feminists have wished to stress not the similarities of men and women, and their entitlement to the same rights, but their differences. These actual differences have not, however, on the whole been used to develop alternative accounts of the rights of women. One reason for this has been that those who affirm the ways in which women are different from men also often stress that they differ in their moral categories or "voice." They claim not (or not only) that women have been denied their rights, or that they should have some alternative set of rights, but that the rhetoric of rights uses a strident and inappropriate ethical register, and may even be seen as an aspect of the oppression rather than the liberation of women. Some radical feminist writing of the last 15 years has criticized concern with justice, hence with rights, as an abstract, adversarial, "male" concern, and has affirmed a conception of ethical life that centres on certain "female" virtues of care and concern, of responsibility and affiliation. Quite a lot of this writing has suggested that we must choose between these ethical voices or stances, that we must choose between justice (and with it obligations and rights) and care and concern, in short that justice and the virtues are the focus of antagonistic rather than of complementary visions of human life.[5]

The worry that we will be forced to this painful choice has a number of sources. One is the lurking belief (mentioned earlier), that just as all rights need corresponding obligations, so all obligations need corresponding rights. If all obligations were the counterparts of rights, then it seems that no discussion of obligations *could* have anything to say about the virtues, about care and concern and the other matters which so many feminists, and so many virtue ethicists, have properly insisted are ethically important: for these can surely not be claimed as a matters of right.

But why should one look at things in this way? While there may be many obligations to which rights correspond, why should there not be many others to which no rights correspond? The traditional distinction between *perfect* or *complete* obligations with counterpart rights, and *imperfect* or *incomplete* obligations without counterpart rights of any sort reminds us that many historically important discussions of human obligations have not restricted themselves to the domain of obligations to which rights are supposed to correspond.[6] There may, for example, be obligations to show others care and concern whose recipients are not specified, and which are to be met by showing *some* others *some* appropriate form of care and concern. Such obligations could not be a matter of providing all possible care and concern to all others, which is impossible. They are inevitably selective. If on the other hand, like so much writing on justice, we treat rights as the basic ethical category, then obligations without rights may simply be overlooked, and it may seem that all virtues must be wholly optional excellences.[7]

However, the fact that obligations with rights may not be the whole story does not mean that they are unimportant, or specifically that they are unimportant for women. To neglect obligations with corollary rights in a discussion of women's issues is no mere oversight. In a world in which women, like men, act and are acted on by the multiple complex institutions and systems of institutions, and by many distant strangers, a pretence that their significant ethical relations are entirely face-to-face, entirely a matter of virtuous relationships, of personal attachments and commitments, of care and concern, and never a matter of required action, of obligations or of rights, is both illusory and dangerous.

The danger is perhaps readily overlooked because the vision of women as using a distinct ethical "voice" or register, which stresses care rather than justice, virtues rather than rights, is coupled with a (sometimes tacit) assumption that women still, at any rate more than men, lead their lives in a "private" sphere whose central ethical categories are appropriately those of virtue rather than of justice. This assumption is false for two distinct reasons. First, it is straightforwardly false of many women, particularly in the developed world, that many, let alone all, aspects of their lives are lived in anything that could be called a private sphere. Labour-force participation rates, voting patterns and dependence on publicly provided support systems all show that women's lives are no longer ensconced, either cosily or uncomfortably, in any private domain, particularly in the developed world. The second reason why the assumption that women's lives are not insulated from the public sphere is false is that no supposedly private sphere is so insulated from the impact of public forces and activities. Economic, political and social forces shape and often grind all private spheres. Economic forces sustain or impoverish families and communities; political realities destroy or enable intimate and personal relationships. This is as true of undeveloped as of developed societies. The only worlds in which it may not have been true are those archaic, or at any rate obsolescent, worlds which lack any clear distinction between public and private domains—the worlds of true *Gemeinschaft*. In the worlds in which we now live women may have somewhat different lives from men, but often the difference is simply that they have more sustained real responsibility for real dependents—for children, for the seriously ill, for the elderly—although they remain economically and socially less powerful.[8] In such worlds it is mere fantasy that a private sphere provides a protective retreat which makes ordinary, mundane rights redundant.

Real Patriarchy?

Yet the image of a sheltered space within which domestic and personal life can be insulated from the pressures of the public domain, and the virtues can flourish, has deep appeal. Perhaps its appeal has increased as the economic, social, political and cultural forces which bear on our lives are increasingly globalised. If we imagine a world in which this sheltered space is peculiarly the domain of women, in which men shelter women from the ravages of the public domain, we are drawn less to the image of *Gemeinschaft* than to the image of *Real Patriarchy*.

The proponents of women's distinctive ethical voice are not, of course, keen on patriarchy of any sort. Yet only patriarchy offers women any prospect of the very insulation from public forces whose attractions seem so persistent to those who emphasize the distinctiveness of women's moral voice and vision. Real patriarchy should at least then be taken seriously, if only because real patriarchs have, or at least had, real obligations, which could provide something worth having—if at a cost. However, all that remains of patriarchy (at least in the developed world) are remnants of patriarchal sentiment and rhetoric without much in the way of patriarchal obligations. The evidence that there isn't much real patriarchy around in the developed world can can be readily assembled by any woman who demands that her male relatives shoulder the obligations of ptriarchy, for example by providing her with a suitable husband or life-long subsistence, or by forcing an erring husband back onto the straight and narrow. Since these fruits of real patriarachy are rarely on offer, the private sphere is unlikely to offer women the securities that supposedly make justice dispensable. Even those who cling to the rhetoric of patriarchy do not now often care to shoulder its obligations; if they try to they are likely to find that the powers and protected spaces by which and in which those obligations could be discharged are no longer available. Would-be patriarchs are almost bound to be frustrated—and probably bit touchy. Even the remnant patriarchs who survive in less developed corners of the world are increasingly powerless to protect women under their sway from larger economic, political and social forces; soon they too may find themselves with too little power to fulfil the obligations of patriarchy.

Yet it surely cannot be a matter for serious regret that there are now no well-insulated private spheres, that real patriarchy is no longer an option, and hence that there is nowhere in which women can cultivate their gardens and the virtues without worrying about justice and rights. If the remnant patriarchs are impotent, the rights and obligations of the public domain can hardly be irrelevant to women; and if they are powerful, but unaccountably so, they will present other dangers, and once again the rights and obligations of the public domain can hardly be irrelevant to women. In either case, reasons for thinking that rights are irrelevant to women or that men and women should have fundamentally different sets of rights are lacking.

If women's rights are not redundant in our world, we need to ask what it would be to take them seriously. I have argued that taking them seriously is preeminently a matter of taking the obligations which are their counterparts seriously. Since rights may be of various sorts, so too may obligations. The obligations that correspond to liberty rights fall on all, and so on women as much as on men, on men as much as on women. By contrast some of the obligations which correspond to rights to goods and services remain amorphous until one or another institutional scheme is established. What matters for women is that the allocation of those obligations to provide goods and services should itself take account of the real resources and responsibilities, of the real capabilities and vulnerabilities, of those who are to bear the obligations. As long as some people, and today it is often (but by no means always) women, and especially poor women in poor economies, have fewer resources and carry higher burdens of dependency, as long as they are vulnerable in ways in which others are not, a case may be made for allocations of obligations which fall rather more on those who have more resources or carry lower burdens of dependency and consequently have greater capabilities. This, however, is not a case for differential rights for women, except in the area of maternity services and the like. It is a case for allocations of obligations to deliver goods and services that take account of the realities of different sorts of lives.

Notes

1. The only exceptions are those unprotected rights which are sometimes spoken of as *mere liberties*. For example, I may have a right which is a mere liberty to pick up a coin from the pavement, and so may you, and neither of us will then have any obligation to let the other exercise the right: The finder may be the keeper. This is a quite different from my having a *claim right* to pick up the coin,

which you have an obligation to respect—even if you find the coin first. The rights that are most important to us are not mere liberties but claim rights with corresponding obligations. I shall say no more about those rights which are mere liberties in this lecture.

2. Regulations requiring prison staff in the UK to shackle pregnant prisoners when in labour were rescinded after public outcry during the winter of 1995–1996.

3. This argument to show that universal rights to goods or services are coherent is intended only to dispose of libertarian allegations that there cannot be such rights, and not to establish which rights to goods or services there may be.

4. For example, Henry Shue in *Basic Rights: Subsistence Affluence and U.S. Foreign Policy* (Princeton: Princeton University Press, 1980).

5. The best-known feminist work on these themes advocates an ethic of care rather than an ethic of justice and rights. See in particular Carol Gilligan, *In a Different Voice: Psychological Theory and Women's Dependence*, 2d ed. (Cambridge: Harvard University Press, 1993). For reasons for thinking that justice and virtue are complementary rather than antagonistic, see Onora O'Neill, *Towards Justice and Virtue: A Constructive Account of Practical Reasoning* (Cambridge: Cambridge University Press, 1996).

6. For an account of traditional (especially early modern) views on justice and virtue that brings out these points, see J. B. Schneewind, "The Misfortunes of Virtue," *Ethics* 101 (1990):42–63.

7. In fact there is no reason to expect that all virtues will be of one kind. Some might be a matter of requirement, even if not owed either to all or to some, hence without counterpart rights. Others might be entirely optional, hence in no way obligatory, a fortiori not claimable as a matter of right.

8. For an account of women's lives and especially of mothering which acknowledges these stark realities, see Sara Ruddick, *Maternal Thinking: Towards a Politics of Peace* (Boston: Beacon, 1987).

3

Are Women Human?

Marilyn French

Major human rights organizations have recently accepted the proposition that women's rights are human rights. This acceptance is a matter for celebration for those of us who care about human rights and those who suffer their infringement. The reason women have had to fight so long for this recognition is that the matter of rights is grounded in a more profound question: whether women are human.

Although the humanity of both sexes seems self-evident, male thinkers have denied female humanness for millennia. The notion of female subhumanness is rooted in the involuntary nature of female biological processes. Male biological processes are of course just as involuntary, but male thinkers ignore or deny this, claiming that males can transcend biological processes. Almost all the literature of the past and much of that of the present—in philosophy, poetry, history, theology, medicine, or science—is haunted by men's demonstrations of male transcendence and female inferiority. In response, women have argued for their humanness in writing at least since the fourteenth century, and Christine de Pisan.

But the argument has not ceased. In 1919, the young Mao-Zedong, not yet a Marxist, wrote nine impassioned articles about Chao wu-chieh, a young woman who stabbed herself to death in her wedding chair. Protesting the marriage system which had almost trapped Mao himself, the articles constitute the first evidence of his rebellion and initiated the May Fourth movement. But he could not argue for changes in marriage law without in some way proving that women are part of *gen*—the human race—an idea that seems to contradict his readers' opinions.

Indeed, this proposition is still not universally acknowledged. Although most people, if queried by a polltaker, would probably assign women human status, many simultaneously feel that women "belong" to men, and that it is right and proper for men to have authority over them. If few people would state explicitly that women are men's property, many betray such a belief in statements about how women should dress and behave, or where they may properly go. There are women as well as men who feel that women should restrict their appearances in public space, that they should not, for instance, walk on city streets at night, and that if they do, they are "asking" for rape or worse. In some countries, women are sometimes molested or splashed with acid because they appear unveiled or unescorted on public streets. In Egypt and Brazil, men consider women who take subways to work to be "asking" to be molested. Everyday, everywhere, churches, nations, institutions, and individuals deny women human status. I will describe some of these denials.

The Denial of Human Rights to Women

The major churches, or organized religions, of the world encompass more territory and more people than any nation state; thus they wield huge influence. And every one of them is built on the presumption that women are less than fully human. Some religions rule on the inheritance of property. Hinduism, for instance, grants female children the right to inherit only in the absence of a male child. Islam grants females the right to inherit, but only half as much as males. Hinduism and the ancestor worship of old China deny females rights on the ground that they cannot perform funerary rites for their fathers. Yet it is religious law that decrees that inability.

Hinduism holds that women are not capable of *moksha* (final salvation). Thus, it is not necessary for them to read religious documents. But what is not necessary in one breath becomes a ban in the next: so, women are forbidden to learn Sanskrit or read the Vedas. Some Hindu laws allow corporal punishment of wives, while others discourage it, but Hindu girls are taught to regard their husbands as gods, and may not remarry if they are widowed. This law is crueller than it sounds. Girls were often married to much older men. If they were widowed in their teens or twenties, they were doomed to spend the rest of their lives in utter destitution, dependent on and abused by their deceased husband's family. Many Hindu wives were kept in seclusion, and few females were trained to support themselves. One can still see aging, hungry, despised widows working in India's agricultural villages. Given the life they were doomed to, it is understandable that widows were willing to commit *sati*—being burned on their husband's funeral pyres—an act that was, and still is, highly praised. Although *sati* is rare today, it is not rare for Indian women to be burned in so-called dowry deaths.

In principle, Islamic law allows daughters to inherit; in practice, they rarely do. The Qur'an, a collection of Muhammad's revelations, contains only a few prescriptions for the imprisonment of wives within clothing or the house, and does not bar them from worshipping at the mosque. But generations of commentators encrusted Muslim practice toward women with greater and greater restrictions, so that by the thirteenth century, it was decreed that women might not display their faces, hands, or any other part *"because the whole body of the free woman is pudendal."* Some Muslim women are still confined in portable tents, and many mosques bar them.

Purdah rules began to loosen in the twentieth century, under Western influence, until the 1979 Shi'ite revolution in Iran. The first actions of the new ruler, the Ayatollah Khomeini, dealt with women. Khomeini immediately abolished women's rights and executed women who had fought for them. In December 1979, Farrokhrou Parsa, a Cabinet member who had directed that school girls need not veil and had established a commission to revise textbooks to present a nonsexist image of women, was accused of "expansion of prostitution, corruption on earth, and warring against God." Tried by judges in hoods, allowed no defense attorney and no appeal, she was declared guilty before the proceedings began. To execute her, Khomeini had her wrapped in a sack and machine gunned.

In 1981, Khomeini had thousands of females, including fifty schoolgirls, arrested and shot for "counter-revolutionary" or "anti-Islamic" activity. None was given a trial; reports indicate that 20,000 women—pregnant, old, and young—were executed. In 1982, Khomeini set the legal minimum age for execution at ten years (or puberty) for girls and sixteen for boys; he banned women from most sports events. In 1983, he made veiling compulsory for women.

Inspired by the Shi'ite revolution, militant Muslim Brotherhoods organized in Afghanistan, Algeria, Tunisia, Egypt, and Saudi Arabia. These groups arose mainly in response to the severe socioeconomic problems and political oppression that followed the end of colonization. Many post-liberation leaders tried to revitalize impoverished economies by introducing industrialization. But development along western lines did not improve life for most people. Crowded into cities lacking adequate housing, water, sanitation, and the social institutions to replace lost village networks, they suffered miseries like those which afflicted British workers during the early industrial revolution. Men suffering from social dislocation, high unemployment, and labor conflict were vulnerable to the rhetoric of Muslim Brotherhoods which revived resentment of the west, urging a militant Islam as the only nationalistic movement, the only alternative to westernization. Like Mussolini and Hitler, leaders of Muslim brotherhoods assert a mythic past—an Islamic past—that was "pure" and harmonious and could be restored. Given their rhetoric, you would expect the Brotherhoods' primary target to be industrialism or westernization—and they do attack westernization. But their primary target is women—as if women caused the present problems and changes in female behavior could solve them.

Yet in most Muslim countries, women have little or no voice in government or institutions. Often, they cannot vote, are illiterate and are married very young; in some states, they are their husbands' possessions by law. The Qur'an licenses corporal punishment of wives within limits.

Still, the Muslim Brotherhoods insist that putting women back in purdah, sending them "back to the bag"—as the mujahadeen put it—expelling them from political office, public space, and paid jobs, will solve their societies' economic and social problems. The Brothers beat, molest, arrest, or throw acid in the faces of women who wear western clothes, enter public space, sit alone in cafes or use buses or subways. No Islamic party runs on an anti-woman platform, but all are open about their primary agenda: to force women back into purdah, out of public space and out of the workforce. Afghan mujahadeen refugees in Peshawar destroyed charitable institutions designed to aid women, and threatened, disappeared, and killed working women. The triumph of the Taliban party has not ended the internecine struggle among Afghani groups, but it has established total subjugation of women, who are now denied education, work, and medical care (except by females—but women have been expelled from schools).[1] They may not leave their houses without a male escort, and must wear "the bag," the huge unwieldly *burqa*.

The idea that subjugating and confining women can create harmony and justice is irrational to the point of insanity. But Islam is not alone in this insanity. Hitler and Mussolini also placed limits on women's rights as an essential part of their political programs. And Western religions follow the same pattern.

The impetus to the rise of American Protestant fundamentalism in the nineteenth century was misogyny.[2] A new generation of ministers rebelled against a church female-led by default. They touted "virile, muscular" Christianity, and demanded that women be ousted from positions of power in church hierarchies and the family. The drive to restore full female subordination remains on the agenda of twentieth-century fundamentalism. Fundamentalists oppose legal abortion, sex education, and shelters for victims of male violence and rape. They call themselves profamily, but the family they favor is the unbreakable nuclear family in the firm control of a man with near-absolute power. Twentieth-century American Protestant fundamentalism is also anti-Semitic (but pro-Israel), often racist, and opposes gun control laws.

But it is most dangerous because of its vaulting ambition. Richard Viguerie, a major strategist of the religious new right, has said, "We've already taken control of the conservative movement. And conservatives have taken control of the Republican Party. The remaining thing is to see if we can take control of the country." When Paul Weyrich was director of the Committee for the Survival of a Free Congress, he said, "We're radicals working to. . . . Christianize . . . America."

Early Christianity preached equality. Jesus taught that women, working men, and publicans were capable of salvation, repudiating the Pharisaic notion that salvation required animal sacrifice in the temple (which only wealthy land-owning men of leisure could perform). Paul preached, "There is neither Jew nor Greek, there is neither slave nor free, there is neither male nor female; for you are all one in Christ Jesus." Women like Prisca of Corinth and Thecla of Iconium were prominent in propagating the new religion—sixteen of the thirty-six founders of new churches who corresponded or travelled with Paul were women. Women supported early Christianity as teachers and priests, saints and martyrs. They founded monasteries and headed double convents, governing monks, nuns, and huge numbers of serfs. They helped to keep education, medicine, art, and drama alive in Europe during harsh times. They had great powers—they were even papal surrogates—until the late twelfth century.

Even before Roman Catholicism was a lawful religion, however, some male leaders tried to curtail female powers, especially of women in gnostic sects. Sexual equality was soon deferred to the afterlife. After its establishment as a state religion in the fourth century, most male Church leaders regarded women as secondary to men, and sometimes as closer to the devil than deity. The struggle against female power within the Church was waged intermittently because some male leaders were inspired and supported by women. But by the fourteenth century, the church had suppressed all female influence, expelling wealthy female patrons as well as priests' wives (who were extremely active, useful, and therefore influential in their parishes). Aristocratic abbesses with intellectual, political, or practical powers were silenced when nuns were confined to the cloister. Such actions reflected the basic principles of a religion founded on the mystery of the Trinity, which symbolically usurps female powers of conception and parturition, attributing them to a male god.

The men of the Catholic church won their struggle against women long ago, but they do not relax their guard. Their most recent war is against abortion. For centuries, abortion was considered wrong mainly because it concealed real sins: adultery and fornication. Abortion was punished less severely than illicit sex, bribery, theft, or divination. Canon law decreed abortion homicide only after the fetus was formed—at forty days for males, ninety for females—until 1917, when Pius IX directed that all abortion be punished by excommunication. But the church almost never baptizes fetal miscarriages or even full-term stillborn babies, and did not pay much attention to abortion until 1968, when feminism had become highly visible and vocal, and women were beginning to demand rights over their own bodies. The Church today wages furious campaigns to criminalize abortion in the United States and Canada, and to keep it illegal in Latin countries. It has found especially fertile ground in former iron curtain countries. New all-male organizations such as Opus Dei function to coordinate these campaigns, which finance anti-abortion activities, even by fundamentalist Protestants.

The strength and effectiveness of Jewish women in founding Israel and the kibbutz system, may mislead us into believing Jewish women have full human rights. But Israeli law is based on the Halachi, religious law codified in the eleventh century, which treats women as male possessions. An Israeli woman cannot divorce unless her husband chooses to release her, even if he has abandoned her and her children and refuses to support them. The education, military training, wages, and political rights of Israeli women are all second-class. Although the low status of women is rooted in a religious document, and Israel is putatively not a theocracy, officials of state—the Knesset and the government—adamantly resist feminist efforts to change the law.

Churches are not alone in trying to fix women in sub-human status. Men in every kind of institution including the family fight relentlessly against female integrity. So fierce is this war and so widespread that women, who until a few years ago comprised the majority of the human race—51 percent—do so no longer.[3]

Everywhere, men impede women from participating in government. In non-industrial countries where women are represented at all, they hold about 6 percent of legislative seats; in European nations, they hold 5–11 percent. In India's last election, women won 7.9 percent of the lower house and about 10 percent of the upper house of Parliament. In the supposedly female-dominated United States, women make up 10.8 percent of the House and only 8 percent of the Senate.

Economic bias against women is even more devastating. United Nations statistics show that women do most of the work in the world—two-thirds to three-fourths of it—producing 45 percent of the world's food. But they earn only 10 percent of the world's income and own 1 percent of its property—and that 1 percent includes male ownership hidden for tax purposes. And this situation is worsening because the global economic system is empowering men in places where women had some traditional powers. Workers once autonomous and isolated are now, for good or ill, linked by the cash crops they raise and the fertilizers they must buy, to the caprice of global markets.

The entire world is linked today by economics, world-scale trading. All states are part of a world market controlled by global agencies—the World Bank, the International Monetary Fund (IMF), and the United Nations (UN). The annual reports of these bodies and of national governments are based on national statistics, the Gross Domestic Product (GDP) or Gross National Product (GNP), which supposedly represent a country's economic performance. These reports are used by aid programs, corporations, and national and international planners; they are the basis of the economy of the future. Men make most of the decisions based on these reports, which *omit the environment, women, and children.*

Making weapons counts as a plus in economic reports, but a tree standing in a forest, combatting erosion, maintaining air quality, providing shade and beauty *does not count*. A tree is worth zero unless it is cut down. And women's great consuming labor of reproducing and maintaining the human race, work that occupies most women for most of their lives, is *specifically excluded* from both GDP and GNP statistics.

For example, consider the Beti of the Cameroon rain forest. Beti men, who raise cocoa, a cash crop and major export, work seven and a half hours a day. They average under an hour a day clearing fields for the women, two hours raising cocoa, four hours making beer, palm-wine, or baskets, or building or repairing houses, making simple commodities for use or sale, or in part-time wage work. The women—women are the farmers in most of Africa—cultivate four to six fields of groundnuts, cassava, cocoyams, plantain and vegetables to feed their families and market locally. Beti women work *at least* eleven hours a day: five hours raising food to eat, another hour to produce a surplus for city markets; three to four hours daily processing and cooking food for the family, and two hours or more collecting water and firewood, washing, tending the children and the sick. Without women's work, the Beti could not live. Yet the International Labor Organization, a UN agency, counts Beti men but not women as "active laborers" because the woman does not "help . . . the head of the family in *his* occupation."

In addition, men in developing societies tend to keep most of their wages for themselves. Studies show that when women have resources or earn income, children are better fed and educated. When men are given new technology to raise cash crops, they earn more money, but give less support to their families, spending more on themselves. Women's and children's nutritional levels fall; women may well do much of the work of raising these cash crops, but the income from them belongs to the men. And men throw "prestige feasts," buy motor-cycles or transistor radios. In Kenya, they gamble, buy liquor, and rent prostitutes while their families starve.[4] In India, men spend about 80% of their earnings on themselves, on toys: motorcycles, radios, wristwatches, television sets, movies, alcohol, and prostitutes. African migrant workers send home on average 10 percent of their earnings. In the United States, 75 percent of divorced men spend more of their incomes on themselves, abandoning their families—yet society blames the mothers, forced onto welfare.

The majority of women in the world work harder than men but few earn cash. And if they do not earn cash, their work is valued less than men's or not at all. Because women are almost never paid for their work in the family, their work is not respected. In many places, even women's work outside the family is not called work. And in many places, when women do waged work, men take women's wages for themselves. If women do not earn wages, they can't buy land, qualify for loans or aid programs. The result in Africa is widespread famine—women can no longer feed their children because the family land is given over to the men's cash crops.

The result in the United States is that four-fifths of the poorest people are women and children, many of them formerly middle class. Most women in industrialized countries work for wages and spend an additional fifty-six hours a week on the vital but unpaid task of reproducing, and maintaining and refreshing the family. But what isn't paid doesn't count. An American woman who works without pay is left destitute, lacking even social security, if her husband divorces her late in life—as many do.

The dire state of the world arises from a system that puts little or no value on peace or preserving natural resources or women's labor in reproducing and maintaining the human race. Indeed, a revealing indication of the values of the men who created this global system is that to increase cash income in poor countries, they invented sex-tourism, tours for men to Third-World brothels built especially for them, womaned by virtual slaves—children sold into servitude by poor peasant fathers. Tourism—which came to include sex-tourism—was proposed as a development strategy by international aid agencies—the World Bank, the IMF and US AID.[5]

All institutions—everywhere—discriminate against women. In education, law, medicine, corporate society, from teachers to police to judges and medical doctors, women receive second-class treatment. In schools, papers bearing female names get lower grades than the same paper delivered under a male name.[6] Teachers of coed classes give two-thirds of their attention to boys, yet they and their students think girls and boys are treated alike. If girls get even 40 percent of the attention, boys usually complain.[7] Add to this a curriculum dominated by (white) male-centered, male-exalting works, and you understand why girls in the United States who are confident and assertive at nine emerge from adolescence with pitiably low self-esteem and the paradoxical fact that in general, the more education women have, the lower their self-esteem.[8]

Many studies of legal systems in some of the United States demonstrated bias against women across the board; women's second-class treatment in medical experiment and expenditure have been widely discussed. I am sure British women have the same experience. Male workers harass and molest women on the job: the major cause of death of women workers in the US is *homicide*. Indeed, huge numbers of women are murdered everywhere: through genital mutilation imposed on over twenty million women worldwide, through selective abortion of an estimated hundred million female fetuses in Asia and China, and the abandoning of girl babies who are born; through the burning of hundreds of thousands of Indian brides so men can get a new wife and another dowry; through legal murder of wives as a crime of honor in places like Brazil.[9]

Across the globe, men beat and rape women and children, intimates and strangers. In the United States, a man beats a woman every twelve seconds. Every day four women are beaten to death by their companions. Officials impatiently tell women to leave brutal men, but Department of Justice statistics show that 75 percent of reported assaults against female companions occur *after* separation. A woman is raped in the United States every three minutes, and rape is increasing.[10] We are only beginning to plumb the dimensions of incest.

How Women Have Fought Back

A massive, cohesive, interlocking structure has kept women-as-a-caste silent for several millennia. But women do not accept victimization silently: they find ways to persuade, negotiate, manipulate, and resist. Since the French Revolution, women have organized politically to struggle for human rights. They have joined together across class, color, religious, and national barriers.

In India, where women are more oppressed by a combination of poverty and male domination than perhaps anywhere else in the world, upper class women have more status than perhaps anywhere else in the world. Many elite Indian women have made extraordinary efforts at outreach. Ela Bhatt for instance founded SEWA, the Self-Employed Women's Association, which organizes women in informal vocations. It offers women training and credit and eliminates the exploitive middlemen who sell their work. SEWA's help is especially useful to women who are confined and work alone at home, easing their isolation and increasing their profits. SEWA has financed thousands of women in small businesses, and women have repaid it at a rate of about 95 percent.

Educated young Indian women founded *Saheli* (female friend), a Delhi collective, to teach women their legal rights and help them find paid work, especially when they decide to divorce. Battered women and girls being forced into unwelcome marriages fleeing to them for asylum transformed Saheli into a shelter. Saheli also performs street plays about women's rights. Women's groups in other states too use this method of reaching illiterate people who rarely encounter radio or television: one based in Tamil Nadu offers skits on wife beating and the enormous burden of women's daily life—fetching wood, fuel, and water, doing field work, cooking, child care. Saheli also organizes charivaris, demonstrating in front of the houses of families who have murdered their daughters-in-law, and at legal courts, to pressure judges to take dowry deaths seriously. Other young elite women go into the countryside to live in small agricultural communities. They live the harsh, primitive life to try to gain the trust of village women, then help them to unite, discover a voice, name their needs, and obtain them.

In the 1970s, during a famine in Maharashtra, leftist women organised lower middle-class and poor women to protest price rises, adulteration, and cheating at ration shops. Thousands demonstrated with rolling pins and brooms. Tribal women organized to protest economic exploitation and sexual harassment by prosperous men and alcoholism and wife-beating by their own men. One of the most brilliant campaigns women initiated in this period was the "Chipko" (hug the trees) movement, which grew into a widespread and well-organized ecological movement.[11]

At the earliest UN Conferences on Women, female African officials refused to discuss female genital mutilation and condemned its discussion by western feminists as patronizing and arrogant cultural colonialism. But in time the UN conferences succeeded in bringing women together, mainly because of informal meetings of women in NGO forums. These meetings have contributed to the rise of a global feminist movement which has been highly effective in Third-World countries. Female doctors and health workers throughout Africa have organized locally and work to end clitoridectomy and infibulation.

Among the educated people who returned from exile after the civil war following Idi Amin's brutal rule, were women attorneys who started the Uganda Association of Women Lawyers and a Women's Legal Aid Clinic.[12] Female lawyers visit rural villages to teach women their legal rights. Most rural women are illiterate, and do not know that wife-beating has been made illegal or that the old form of marriage is no longer valid. Unless a marriage is recognized by the state, the husband's family can seize all his assets after his death, leaving his wife and children penniless.

In fighting for their own rights, women often fight for the human rights of men. Women in racist countries have long been involved in building bridges between colors, and fighting for the rights of the disfranchised. The US women's movement grew out of the nineteenth-century abolition movement, in which women were profoundly engaged. Lucretia Mott, a feminist hero, was also a daring participant in the Underground Railroad. Twentieth-century feminists have made strong efforts to link up with African-American women, not always successfully.

White women like Ruth First and Helen Joseph made remarkable efforts against racism in South Africa, and some white groups organized to work against white privilege, in sympathy for black female workers. In the 1930s, some trade unions organized; after the Afrikaner Nationalist Party won the 1948 election and installed apartheid, trade union members joined the massive multiracial nonviolent resistance movement. At a tea party in 1955, a group of white housewives risked ostracism and jail by organizing. Alarmed at African Nationalist Party efforts to erode the already limited franchise of Coloured men, they founded the Women's Defence of the Constitution League. They kept vigil at government offices, despite rocks, garbage, and threats hurled at them by Afrikaner men; they wore black sashes to mourn the "death" of the Constitution, and later took the name Black Sash. Their activities were universally scorned: by United States standards they were conservative; for white South Africans they were radical; and for African militants they were hopelessly ineffective.

Women in India, Lebanon, Israel, and elsewhere, have risked imprisonment and death in their efforts to heal factional or religious divisions. Feminists in the New Delhi Ankur project helped the widows of Sikh men killed by Hindus in the riots that followed Indira Ghandi's assassination. As civil war wracks Sri Lanka, Women for Peace organize northern Tamil and southern Sinhalese women, circulate peace petitions, hold public meetings, and publish news-letters criticizing government policy.

Isolation within sectarianism increases the likelihood of conflict among groups. Such isolation is worse for women than men if women are confined or kept under surveillance. In India, I observed the skittishness of women at local wells, who apparently feared to be observed conversing with each other. An Indian UNICEF official told me that when a development group erected walled privies in his mother's village, she—who lived in confinement—lost her one chance of conversation with other women. Women could converse only when, as he put it, they squatted.

The first UN World Conference for Women in Copenhagen in 1980 gave women across the world an opportunity to converse across religious and factional lines. Afterwards, women made daring efforts to build bridges to peace. Women deserve part of the credit for ending the factionalist war that raged among Christians, Muslims, and Druzes (with intervention by Israel and Syria) in the once beautiful Lebanese city of Beirut from 1975 to 1991. Lebanese women's lives are regulated by the laws of their religious communities, not national laws. But these communities are insular and keep people from talking to each other. After the Copenhagen Conference, Lebanese women formed inter-denominational groups that organized peace marches, sit-ins, and hunger strikes. Standing defiantly between the guns of the divided city, they appealed to fighters by visiting refugee camps and military headquarters and sticking flowers in gun nozzles. To eliminate militia checkpoints where people were kidnapped, they went from East to West Beirut, from Phalangist to Progressive checkpoint, begging men in the name of their wives, mothers, and sisters, to stop the butchery. They blocked passageways dividing the two sides of the capital, led all night sit-ins, and stormed local TV stations, interrupting the news to broadcast their demands. In May 1984, they held a peace march that included women from both sides of the city, who were to meet at the only crosspoint, the Museum passage. They were halted by a "blind" shelling—a randomly aimed barrage—that killed and wounded women from both sides.[13]

In contravention of Israeli law, Israeli women met with Palestinian women; they held peace demonstrations in the streets, where passing Israeli men cursed and stoned them. In December 1989, Israeli, Palestinian, and European women held a large joint peace march from west to east Jerusalem. As they entered a courtyard, someone (probably not a marcher) raised a Palestinian flag, which was outlawed in Israel. The police erupted, hitting the women with sticks, kicking them, dragging them by their hair. They even fired tear gas at the 3000 women marching for peace.[14]

Peace is pre-eminently a women's issue, and everywhere, women are in the forefront of movements for peace and against militarism and nuclear power. Women's groups in Europe, North America, and Australia have often protested nuclear energy, weapons, and—during wars—held anti-war demonstrations. South Pacific women in the Nuclear Free Pacific Movement tried to stop nuclear testing there—successfully until France's recent outrageous breach. Nowhere did women campaign as indefatigably against the nuclear arms race as in England. They helped mount the 1980s Campaign for Nuclear Disarmament, but their most famous peace action is Greenham Common. This movement arose in response to the 1979 announcement by NATO that it would place hundreds of American nuclear missiles in Western Europe, broadly intensifying the nuclear arms race. The first installation of ninety-six ground-launched Cruise missiles was planned for 1983 at a US air base at Greenham Common. In response, forty British women walked 120 miles from Wales to Greenham Common in September 1981, protesting and publicizing this use of British soil.[15] Hundreds, even thousands of women joined them over the years, and Greenham inspired similar encampments in Europe and the US.

A major accomplishment of feminism has been to bring to light the facts of male abuse. Men have beaten, molested, imprisoned, raped, tortured and murdered children, wives and lovers for millennia. In past societies, indeed until the feminist movement of the nineteenth century, men's right to perform such acts was specified by law (as it still is in some places). Even after such laws were rescinded, women rarely got help from police or social agencies and could not escape from abusive mates unless their families were sympathetic. All families were not sympathetic, but even when they were, sometimes enraged men killed the entire family. Sexual assault of children was a taboo subject, precluding legal or psychological actions against it. It has since come out into the open, although no society I know of has figured out a decent institutional method of dealing with it.

Women fight back against physical abuse: every year, 500–750 American women kill battering men. Forty percent or more of women who kill do so in self-defense. Such women—who openly admit their acts—have usually been sentenced to life imprisonment. This is particularly ironic, since in the US, the average sentence given men for murder is something like seven years. But about a decade ago *for the first time* feminist lawyers in the United States began to plead self-defense for such women.[16] Some women were acquitted on this defense; and some who were imprisoned won new trials or reviews and were released from jail. In 1990 and 1991, some state governors granted clemency or commuted the sentences of women convicted of the murder of battering husbands. Women's and criminal justice groups are working across the US to pass laws explicitly allowing battered women charged with violence against their abusers to introduce evidence of their abuse and its psychological effects in their defense. Several states have passed such laws. Of course, there is also a men's group fighting this.

Global feminist organizations have been formed, like DAWN, Development Alternatives with Women for a New Era, an India-based international organization that connects Third-World women activists, researchers, and policy makers developing a global perspective on women's economic and political situation.[17] In cities across the world women have created shelters for battered women, displaced homemakers, and rape victims. In Southeast Asia, women organized projects to assist victims of battery and rape but also to change rape laws and community attitudes. Indian women bang pots and pans outside the houses of men who are particularly abusive to their wives, and agitate against "dowry deaths." Their pressure forced passage of a law requiring any "accidental death" or "suicide" of a woman in the first seven years of her marriage to be investigated for possible foul play. In the US, women's organizations try to provide a safe house, food, and clothing for battered women and their children, a safe haven for rape victims, counseling and re-training for displaced homemakers. They are forced every year to beg for government money. No government, whatever its character, has been liberal toward such groups, but the present Congress wants to cut off funds to such groups almost entirely.

Until feminism, and the founding of shelters in the late twentieth century, no institutions existed to harbor women victims of male abuse—with only two exceptions that I know of. Australian aboriginal women have a refuge—the *jilimi*, a women's camp. Any woman may visit or reside there, but no man may enter or even pass near it, which may require them to take long, roundabout routes when travelling. The camp is a haven for single women, widows who choose not to remarry, estranged wives of violent husbands, women visiting from other areas, sick women and any dependent children. Married women come for a day's visit; a woman may live in the camp and go home occasionally to spend time with a man or men.

And in Japan during the Kamakura period (1185–1333), women could escape from intolerable marriages by fleeing to a temple that offered sanctuary. There were few such temples, and it might be hard for a woman to reach one. In addition, she had to abandon her children. Escape had to be well planned, because if the husband's servants caught her before she reached sanctuary, she was dragged back. Common law came to hold that a woman who managed to throw her shoe through the gate could not be forced to return home. Once in the temple, after serving in the convent three years, she could petition to be restored to her parents' home. Fugitive wives had to show good cause before the temple would initiate proceedings for them. Interestingly, a recent article on unhappy marriages in Japan pointed out that despite marital misery, there is little divorce. Women are trapped in miserable marriages by economic need. Men are kept in miserable marriages by shame. As one man explained, "If you divorce, you lose face in society. People say, 'His wife escaped.'." It seems little about marriage has changed in Japan over seven hundred years.[18]

In the past two centuries, women—especially educated western women—have expanded their rights. The State of the World's Women Report, issued at the end of the UN Decade for Women in 1985, disclosed that 90 percent of all nations had official agencies dedicated to women's advancement, half created during the decade. At present, UN officials estimate that all countries have them. Before 1974, only twenty-eight states required equal pay for equal work; in 1985, ninety did so. With tremendous effort, particularly by Bella Abzug, the 1994 International Conference on Population and Development in Cairo took a huge step forward and acknowledged that the key to population control was not class but education, not men, but women. For decades, the accepted theory held that raising men's economic status would lead to reductions in family size. Instead, what has been proven to encourage population control is female education and a means of birth control. All the 185 member nations (except Saudi Arabia) signed the UN Convention on the Elimination of all Forms of Discrimination Against Women (CEDAW) at Beijing in 1995. The 1985 CEDAW granted women constitutional and legal equality; the 1995 CEDAW granted women, for the first time in history, rights of possession over their *own* bodies. This is an extraordinary step forward.

In any given nation, these changes may be limited to the paper they're written on, may even disguise a worsening of women's situation. They offer legal tools to forge real change—yet it is not unheard of for signed documents to be put away in drawers to curl up and yellow—or even to remain vital, like the Qur'an, while provisions granting women rights are ignored. Every world religion whose roots we can trace—Christianity, Islam, Protestantism, and offshoots like the Society of Friends—established itself largely by attracting women by preaching sexual equality. And once established, every religion modified or reversed this teaching. The same pattern occurs in secular revolutions. When a revolution seeks adherents, it preaches sexual equality. Some revolutions even tried to honor this promise. Revolutionary governments in Russia, China, and states like Mozambique and Eritrea granted women a number of rights. But these were soon rescinded by fiat, altered, or allowed to rot, unenforced.

During the 1970s, American feminist historians cited periods in history during which women had a considerable voice. They noted that women held positions of power in early Japan and in Hellenistic Greece after the death of Alexander. Women ran the Roman Empire behind the scenes, initiating a period of peace and prosperity lasting several hundred years. In sixteenth-century England, the tradition of *feme sole* allowed married women to do business in their own right; and churchwomen wielded huge powers throughout Christian Europe from the eighth to twelfth centuries. In every such case, however, women lost these powers when men campaigned against them. The historians argued that women's problem was that they always held power informally, and that until their right to a voice, to power, was codified, made law, women's status would remain vulnerable.

Yet women in the United States probably had greater chances for advancement during the seventies and early eighties than they do now. In the last two decades, a silent but seemingly across-the-board collusion has arisen in institutions to ignore or abolish women's rights and women's voice. With the money to back up their desires, male-run institutions can fight the law—as the American Congress is presently trying to do with laws ameliorating poverty and laws granting the right to legal abortion. Even codification is not enough to resist male prejudice.

Women's Rights in the Future

Only in the Scandinavian countries is the status of women higher than in the US. Yet at the end of the twentieth century, the women of the United

States have been unable to enter into the Constitution a sentence declaring them men's equals, with equal rights. It is unlikely that women throughout the world will attain permanent human status without serious study of male thinking and feeling, and a serious effort by men to change their behavior. Men need to look at their condition.

Men are also oppressed. They are oppressed as members of minority groups or groups designated despised—non-Han Chinese, Sikhs, Kurds, Hutu, Tutsi, Jews, Muslims, or Christians, depending on place. Men who are among the billions of the world's poor folk are victimized. Oppression of the poor and of chosen groups is as old as the state. But in a world driven by lust for power—which is inevitably a predatory world—all men, even those of elite classes, suffer victimization as children. In a power-driven society, children, the most powerless members of society are the ultimate victims. I believe that no one in our world—with the possible exception of a few simple societies in the southern hemisphere—grows up ignorant of oppression and victimization. Everyone knows how it feels to be treated as less than human.

The argument has been made that men who suffer discrimination and inequity fight back, rebel against their oppressors, while women do not. Their so-called passivity in the face of oppression is taken as a sign of women's natural inferiority: women are denied rights because they will not fight for them. They deserve their condition. Let's consider this charge.

Men abused as children may accept their brutalization as a necessary step toward manhood, and exalt their torturers, praising the brutal father for righteousness. They know that as adults, they will have similar powers, and they ignore the parts of themselves that are destroyed by childhood abuse. Like most women, they acquiesce to the system, hoping to be assimilated within it. Some men build up a store of hatred, and dream of someday overcoming their oppressor; some men mount personal revolutions, some become outlaws. They may try to escape oppression as individuals, like the Caribbean Maroons. Such men attack the person or class that oppresses them, not the system itself.

When an entire group of men is repressed, it responds according to certain patterns. Some assimilate, then usurp, like the Mamluks of Egypt who, as slaves, became powerful ministers to their masters, but eventually took over the kingdom. Some envision a return to a homeland, or reestablishment of their dominance over that homeland (Israelis and Palestinians, Hutu and Tutsi, Sikhs, Kurds in Turkey and Iraq, or the men of Chechnya, for instance).

Rebellion requires certain conditions. First, a rebel group must create a discrete identity. It does this by banding together and emphasizing the factors the group holds in common. The reasons Africans enslaved in the

US so rarely escaped were, first, refuge was hard to find. The only state on the continent where Africans were free and safe was Florida, a hard-to-reach Spanish colony. Second, most slaves worked in isolation from each other. The stereotype of American slavery is the huge plantation with hundreds of slaves, but in fact most slaves in nineteenth-century America were the single African on a farm. At most, there might be one other who might not even speak the same African language. Slaves unable to talk to each other could not make common cause. In all power cultures, masters fear group solidarity, and forbid vassals to speak to each other—like Indian husbands in rural villages, or foremen in textile sweatshops in Emma Goldman's America—and our own.

The second necessity for rebellion is confidence. The group must see itself as possessing natural strength. Such a self-image can be produced by creating or invoking a hero or a myth of a glorious past, like those invoked by Hitler and Mussolini. On my first visit to Poland, in the early 1980s, I was struck by the great number of huge paintings I saw of a great Polish victory over the German army. It was the *only* Polish victory over the Germans, and it had occurred in the fourteenth century. Morale rose in concentration camps when an inmate committed suicide. By taking action, a person reminded the group it had strength, and became exemplary. Many groups raise their confidence by intensifying male domination of the women of their group.

Third: the oppressor must be demonized, hated passionately. Since the oppressor has superior power and may very well awe the dominated group, it takes time to build enough confidence and hatred to attack it. Uprisings often occur after an oppressor commits some particularly cruel act. Officers may brainwash soldiers into hating the enemy, especially when the so-called enemy has not committed some injustice to initiate the conflict. Brainwashing soldiers was not necessary during World War II, but it was during the Vietnamese war; George Bush demonized Saddam Hussein to legitimate the Gulf war. Soldiers are taught to hate to overcome their fear and sense of vulnerability.

Thus, revolution requires a discrete group with a clear identity; enough confidence to fight; and the kind of clear morality that arises from having a demonized enemy. It is always morally right to kill the devil. When definitions are not clear—as in Yugoslavia or Rwanda and Burundi—they are simplified to seem so. Deviations from the myth are seen as treason.

In this male model of resistance to oppression, rebellions may succeed or not, but the path of resistance is clear. This model is useless for females. In the first place, females are universally oppressed. A woman gains little by escaping from China to the Philippines, assuming she could gain entry. She may gain sanctuary in Canada or Norway or the United States, and suffer from less discrimination than at home, but she will still suffer discrimination as a woman. There is no Florida for women.

Second: women's enemy is their entire culture. They are oppressed by the very context that provides their home and nurturance. Women everywhere are abused by their government—secular rulers they may respect and revere—and their church—clerical authorities who may provide the only solace in their lives. Many women cannot bring themselves to view such authorities as enemies; and those who can face the dilemma of rebelling *without support* against their own institutions and often even against their own friends and kin.

Even when women find ways to unite, to make common cause, even when they raise their confidence by producing a coherent analysis of their oppression, they cannot name a common enemy. Their enemy is men—some of whom they love, who claim to love them and often do—their fathers, husbands, brothers. Yet these same men are sadly also sometimes willing to kill them if they defy the constrictions men have placed upon them. If women do name men their enemy, they feel wrong, because not all men are in fact their enemies. But there is no way to distinguish those who are (or might be in certain conditions) from those who are not. Nor are most women willing to demonize the people they love.

Women must therefore fight in an entirely different way. They fight subtly, sensitively, using their knowledge of psychology and emotion, working around people rather than threatening them with injury or death. This is a difficult form of resistance, and one which often yields small victories. Thus, it is not possible for women globally to realize their full humanity without men's cooperation.

Even a brief glance at some of the forms in which men worldwide deny women human rights forces us to consider male psychology. Why are men-in-general obsessed with dominating women?; and how is it that not all men are? What do men gain from denying women full human status? Some male scientists argue that a drive to dominate women is inherent in male genetic makeup. They are claiming that *nature* programmed half the human species to prey systematically on the other half.

But what can we deduce from the ruins of early societies, like that of Catal Hüyük and other Anatolian towns, in old Europe, ancient Crete, Britain and Malta. Such ruins suggest humans lived in egalitarian societies for thousands of years without war or (in Anatolia and Skara Brae) even rulers, and that women even had a slight edge in status. Was human nature different then? Did our DNA change?

And besides: what happens to a species half of which systematically preys upon the other half and on the very half that takes responsibility for the young of the species? In animal species in which one sex dominates or preys upon the other—like bees, or the praying mantis, for example, or fish in which the male is an appendage to the female, or fish that switch sex at need—the power relation serves to advance the survival of the species.[19] But in our world, male predation on women is endangering not just women, but children, the future of our race, our means of survival.

I cannot believe that nature programs men to be women's enemies. I think hostility between the sexes arose because men, feeling they lacked a given natural role like women's, and seeing that role as a power, attempted to transcend the natural female power of conception and parturition by inventing symbolic forms of power. Resenting the dominant edge of women in pre-historic societies, men manufactured a gender role, defining themselves in opposition to Woman. Because this role is manufactured, not natural, it requires education. So men invented puberty rites, which celebrate a change that is imperceptible and uncertain: the male ability to reproduce, unlike females', is not marked by any visible sign. Some animal species cast out their males at adolescence, but none brutalizes them. Nor do gathering-hunting cultures hold group initiations of males; such rites appear first in horticultural societies where gender roles are easily blurred.

They remain in male-dominated power societies like our own. Nature does not require us to "make a man" of a son by brutalization. Whether in all-male schools, military prep schools or colleges, or military service, men teach boys that males must either brutalize or be brutalized. Men define manhood as superiority to and control of women (and for the elite, manhood requires controlling other men as well). The feminine mystique described by Betty Friedan decades ago has its counterpart in a male mystique the characteristics of which we all recognize. The gender mystiques are fostered early, and are maintained mainly by coercion.

Feminists have deeply considered the effects on their lives of the feminine mystique, but men in general hesitate to consider the price they pay for bowing to the masculine mystique. That price includes sacrificing personal goals and passions to the supposedly masculine goal of instrumental power, adopting a false personality and a false language (a language of symbolic power), and concealing vulnerability, indeed, pretending it does not exist. Men must continually prove their manhood, which requires sacrificing what most women cherish most—hope for a life centered in contentment and affection. Men know that heroes are loners, Shanes riding off alone into the desert, scorning the domestic ideal. Real men are not allowed contentment or happiness.

Yet despite roughly five thousand years of institutionalized male dominance, men have never felt they really controlled women. And no matter how old they grow, they are never relieved from the necessity of proving their "manhood." Trapped in a mystique as delicate and powerful as a spider web (which according to an African proverb, can stop a lion), and believing it to be a biological imperative, men spend their lives seeking power and its symbols, while silently feeling like failures, lonely and misunderstood.

If men made the kind of effort required of women who become feminists, they would enrich their lives. They could distinguish their own needs and wants from those they are taught to value; they could learn to speak and act from desire instead of servilely adopting an image created in resentment and fear. Men do not need to prove their *sex*: men are men simply because they exist. They feel a need to prove their gender—a different quality—but they can define that for themselves. Men and women are cohorts, fellow-sufferers, sharers in a human project—creating felicitous life. The desires of the two sexes are occasionally at cross purposes, but I believe that in their deepest feelings, the two sexes are similar.

I would like to end tonight on a positive note, emphasizing women's victories over oppression, praising women's courage, praising men who have supported women's rights as human rights, and hoping for continued transformation. I would like to end by assuring you—and myself—of a better future. But I cannot. Global feminism is a powerful force, and will continue to transform lives everywhere. But the new world economy bodes ill for most human beings, women and men, as do the supposedly neutral new forms of social control being put into place across the globe. The new global economy subsumes a global politic, involving the creation of a small global elite in possession of 95 percent of the world's resources, a nervous professional class subject to the elite, and a huge global proletariat that lives from hand to mouth. After millennia of revolution against tyrants, feudal lords, and monarchs; after a heaving century of revolution waged at huge sacrifice by workers and women and people of color willing to die to gain their rights, the world seems to be regressing to the political/economic form of the bloody earliest states: a god-king who is also a killer, an elite troop of loyal generals, obsequious priests, and tractable palace officials, and the bondslaves who constitute the majority of the population. All three classes live in fear. Constant fear.

The only politics that offers an alternative to this wretched future is feminism. Women must continue to organize to overcome discrimination and advance their own values. Only by solidarity can women convince men that males bear half the responsibility for raising the next generation of the human race and are profoundly needed in this task. Only if men recognize that they do not have to live in misery, and join with women in resisting the forces that turn human beings into cogs and instruments, do we have a hope of turning away from a power- and profit-oriented morality. Only by organizing politically and electing women to office can we pressure male-dominated governments to recognize that having babies and raising children are the most important human tasks—indeed the only essential human task.

Instead of allocating the bulk of the national budget to armies and weapons whose function is to kill the children of others, governments (especially of the most culpable nation in this regard—the United States) should allocate the major proportion of our resources to supporting those who raise children and guaranteeing every child a safe and healthful place to live, decent food, medical care, education, and opportunities for work. Human necessities are human rights: what we must have, we deserve to have. Together, women and men must work toward a world in which no one dominates anyone, in which no sex, color, religion, or class dominates any other. This can only occur when domination itself is seen as a false idol, a perversion of human good.

This vision is an ideal, a dream. But there is no point and no pleasure in working toward anything less. We aim at an ideal; we achieve what we can. Action is necessary: what is at stake are the largest and smallest elements of human existence—our survival as a race and the possibility of felicity in our personal lives. To fight for human rights is to fight for a human future.

Notes

1. John F. Burns, "From Cold War, Afghans Inherit Brutal New Age," *New York Times*, February 14, 1996.

2. Betty A. DeBerg, *Ungodly Women: Gender and the First Wave of American Fundamentalism* (Minneapolis: Fortress, 1990).

3. See *The World's Women: 1970–1990: Trends and Statistics* (New York: United Nations, 1991).

4. Irene Tinker, "New Technologies for Food-Related Activities: An Equity Strategy," in *Women and Technological Change in Developing Countries*, ed. Roslyn Dauber and Melinda L. Cain (Boulder, Colo.: Westview, 1981).

5. Maria Mies, *Patriarchy and Accumulation on a World Scale: Women in the International Division of Labour* (London: Zed Books, 1986), pp. 137–142.

6. Berit Aangstroms, "The Feminist University," in *Radical Voices: A Decade of Feminist Resistance*, ed. Renate Klein and Deborah Lynn Steinberg, Women's Studies International Forum (Elmsford, N.Y.: Pergamon, 1989). She cites a study done by Phillip Goldberg, "Are Women Prejudiced Against Women?" in *And Jill Came Tumbling After: Sexism in American Education*, ed. Judith Stacey et al. (New York: Dell, 1974); Dale Spender, *Man Made Language* (London: Routledge and Kegan Paul, 1980); Birgit Brock-Utne and Runa Kaukaa, *Kunuskap Uten Maks* (Knowledge without power) (Olso: University Press, 1980).

7. Dale Spender, *Invisible Woman: The Schooling Scandal* (London: Writers and Readers, 1982).

8. The study, commissioned by the American Association of University Women and conducted by Greenberg-Lake Analysis Group, surveyed 2,400 girls and 600

boys at thirty-six public schools in twelve communities throughout the country in 1990. It was reported in the *New York Times*, January 9, 1991.

9. For estimates of the number of women who suffer genital mutilation, see Fran Hosken, *The Hosken Report: Genital and Sexual Mutilation of Females* (Lexington, Mass.: Women's International Network News, 1979); Hanny Lightfoot-Klein, *Prisoners of Ritual: An Odyssey into Female Genital Circumcision in Africa* (New York: Harrington Park, 1989); and Lilian Passmore Sanderson, *Against the Mutilation of Women* (London: Ithaca, 1981). The figure of 100 million babies comes from Amartya Sen, "More Than 100 Million Women Are Missing," *New York Review of Books*, December 20, 1990.

10. Statistics in this paragraph come from Lori Heise, "The Global War Against Women," *Washington Post*, April 9, 1989.

11. Madhu Bhushan, "Vimochana: Women's Struggles, Nonviolent Militancy, and Direct Action in the Indian Context," in *Women's Studies International Forum* 12, ed. Berenice A. Carroll and Jane E. Mohraz (New York: Pergamon, 1989).

12. Jane Perlez, "When the Trouble Is Men, Women Help Women," *New York Times*, June 5, 1989.

13. This was organized by Imam Khalifeh, a kindergarten teacher and member of Beirut University College in West Beirut.

14. "Officers Break Up a March in Israel," *New York Times*, December 30, 1989.

15. Anne Witte Garland, *Women Activists: Challenging the Abuse of Power* (New York: Feminist Press, 1988).

16. The British journalist Beatrix Campbell made a documentary on this subject: *I Killed My Husband . . . and No One Asked Me Why* (London: Scarlet Productions, 1988).

17. Amrita Basu, "Reflections on Forum '85 in Nairobi, Kenya: Voices from the International Women's Studies Community," *Signs,* Spring 1986, pp. 584–608.

18. Nicholas D. Kristof, "Who Needs Love? In Japan, Many Couples Don't," *New York Times*, February 11, 1996.

19. Such as the Caribbean bluehead wrasse, the anemone fish, and the grouper, among others.

4

"Women Are Like Cold Mutton": Power, Humiliation, and a New Definition of Human Rights

Naomi Wolf

Here we are in the Sheldonian—this celebrated jewel box of eighteenth-century British male oratorical treasure. And it is, of course—*of course*—a great honor to be here.

And that—honor—is a sentiment worth looking at in relation to the subject of women and human rights. Tonight I want to talk about the feeling of honor, and about its corollary, that of humiliation; and about how institutions, including this one, use these feelings—consciously or casually, depending upon where you happen to be in the world—in ways designed to keep women outside of that magic circle of those understood to possess fully human status.

This morning, as I walked around the beautiful streets of Oxford, I was overcome with memories of my own time spent as a student here. I remembered, as I walked, the great loveliness of the May morning celebration, with the treble singing of little boys descending from the height of Magdalen tower at dawn like the very voice of tradition; I thought about the gliding of the punts on the Cherwell, and the clatter of shoes as young people in commoner's gowns ran down the worn-away steps after the Latin grace in Hall; I recalled the flash of the deer in the deer park, and the sweet smell of first editions on the shelves of the Bodleian.

But I was also aware that, much as I wanted to on the day I first bought my own second-hand black scholar's gown, and much as I still want to today, I will never be able fully to claim the richness of Oxford as having belonged, if even for a matter of a few years, to me; to me, that is, too.

The reason for that involves these very different memories, which are just as lasting: of having heard of at least two young women who had been stalked here—one by a staff member, one by an undergraduate. Both had to leave their studies in the middle of term because the authorities would do nothing about it. I remember being warned about some professors, whose routine sexual harassment of female students was treated as a subject of Senior Common Room mirth over glasses of sherry—it was considered to be so inconsequential that no one even bothered to call it a secret. Students, as I remember it, did not bother to go through university channels about sexual harassment issues because it was taken for granted that nothing would happen that wasn't more dangerous for the complainant.

I remember quiet conversations among young women huddled over mugs of tea by the electric fires in their graduate quarters far from home: "My adviser is always talking to me, when I am alone in his office, about how attractive Indian women are," said one young woman, an Indian. "The woman appointed to be the liaison at my college to the SCR for women's issues—the senior fellows mock her to her face," said another, an undergraduate.

I recall the rumor that the first class of female undergraduates at Oriel was chosen for their looks—the dons, it was whispered, had reasoned that the prettier girls would have an easier time of it. I recall a don at an SCR dinner informing me in stentorian tones that feminist theory was a contradiction in terms. I vividly recall the bitter fight in my own New College common room when women students argued that communal money should no longer go to subscriptions to tabloids with naked women on page 3—or, if we were to continue with the page 3 girls, there should at least be a subscription to *Ms.* magazine as well. I remember the notice I posted inviting women to discuss this being defaced. I remember it being slashed with pens until the paper tore; I remember it being turned to the wall. I remember the guys on the crew team staking out the common room as territory that was not common at all; I remember them holding aloft the contested newspapers, and loudly counting and evaluating the page 3 nipples as the other young women, their fellow students, were foraging for biscuits and struggling to wake up on cold, hung-over Sunday mornings.

I remember the young women meeting one another's eyes, and looking away, and, ashamed at their silence, saying nothing.

Above all, I remember the cold mutton anecdote. It was the day of my first tutorial, and I was excited. I had worked hard to earn the scholarship that had brought me here, and I felt filled with a sense of anticipation and joy. I felt, in short, as I waited with the other students in the oak-panelled rooms for the tutorial to begin, both honorable and honored.

The tutor, an esteemed scholar and influential member of my faculty's academic hierarchy, gave us his introduction. In it, he mentioned Oscar Wilde. "I am reminded of a joke," he remarked jovially to the seven men and five women seated before him.

It seems that Oscar Wilde confided to a heterosexual friend that he had never had sex with a woman. This friend, a roué, hoping to contribute to Wilde's education, arranged for the writer to have sex with a female prostitute. Wilde did so. "Well, how was it?" pressed his friend. "I must say," reported Wilde—and reported our professor to us—"it reminded me of cold mutton."

Cold mutton.

There were five women in that room. Every one of us possessed the sexual characteristics that had just been compared to cold mutton—a comparison that suggested (for we were, after all, fledgling literary critics) not just an unpleasant quality, but something actively repulsive. Five people in that room had been humiliated sexually, and eight had not. None of us dared to say anything. We understood that if we wanted to be welcomed into this treasure house of all the things we loved, we would need to leave our sexual dignity—indeed, our allegiance to our identity as women—outside the door.

You might think, by the way, that that anecdote was simply an embarrassing slip on the part of the professor. I myself kept hoping that it was. But, before the term was over, he had managed to tell it *again*.

Let us move from Britain's most privileged institution to one that more accurately reflects most British—and, for that matter, American—women's work experience: In Derbyshire this week, two women attended a company dinner at which, they said, a salesman danced with an inflatable sex doll and a woman was forced to sit next to the doll; a woman was presented with a chocolate penis; and a prize was awarded to the "girl"—to use the words of the *Daily Telegraph*—with the biggest breasts. When the women complained, they claimed, they were forced out of their jobs.

The reporting of the event, typically, stressed "humor" as a motivation. "Dirty joke payout" was one headline; "Crude humor," another. Which reinforces the question many legitimately have about such furores: what is the big deal? Why can't these women just laugh it off?

In Indonesia, women are arbitrarily arrested as suspected prostitutes during urban "cleansing" sweeps; they are forced to undergo internal examinations. In Jakarta, two women were examined vaginally during interrogation; two others, waiting for a bus outside a university some time later, were also subjected to vaginal examinations during detention. The examinations are often followed by direct sexual abuse. Amnesty points out that since those arrested are not charged formally and lack access to lawyers—and are sometimes held for up to a year—that these arrests may be being used simply "to intimidate and target women who are out alone at night."

Now, this matter of "offensive" jokes and commentary has precipitated a vast amount of chaotic debate. We still do not know quite what to make of such moments, or what, if anything, should be done about them. Did the joke destroy our "self-esteem?" No; we were tougher than that; to say the least, we lived through it, and even learned something useful about the Georgian poets. Was it a sexual coup for the professor—was he manifesting a sadistic exercise of his patriarchal power that gave him an eroticized thrill? I sincerely doubt it. Should he be fired for it? He was a marvellous exegete; he should not.

But was it an important moment to understand in terms of the just functioning or the profound corruption of institutional activity and social organization—in terms of the corruption of what is acknowledged to be the forcing-house of Britain's elite, and the corruption, eventually, of the institutions which its graduates go on to create and sustain? Yes; it was.

For I am now convinced that those moments in which women are humiliated sexually within institutions go beyond the discourses with which we are familiar—discourses of sexual titillation, and even of patriarchal power. We are often asking the wrong questions about these incursions, whether we call them "sexual harassment" or "campus oversensitivity." We tend to ask: was it offensive? Was it a come-on? Did he mean to offend her? Is she a prude? Was it personal? Instead, we should at least some of the time be asking: was it functional?

The questions we should ask go, that is to say, to the heart of the way human beings construct societies, and either perceive or fail to perceive others as being human too. We need an anthropological understanding of what happens when institutions sanction women's being humiliated sexually.

We must take moments in which institutions use sexual humiliation as a principle of social organization—which is what I think was going on in Derbyshire and in my seminar room, on a lesser point but at the same scale as what happens to women out late in Jakarta—very seriously indeed because they are in fact organizational, not sexual. The "jokes" in question in the Western contexts were all designed to convey to women, and to the men watching and listening, that the women's sexual privacy is conditional and not inviolable. This humiliation has a genuine function within the life of organizations. At the time I was a student eight years ago, there were one and a half female fellows in my college—and forty-nine male fellows. The scholarship I was on had a twenty-year record of the underrepresentation of women. The two facts—the micro moment of sexual humiliation, and the macro status quo of discrimination and exclusion—were related; were functional coefficients. The pro-male bias that was effectively keeping the academic plums for men needed the cold mutton joke to ease its work.

Cross-culturally, as anthropologists point out, one recognized hallmark of humanity is the act of setting—and of having the right to set—boundaries of privacy around one's own body. Conversely, it is also true that, cross-culturally, enforced nakedness is a marker that indicates that one is outside the pale of a given human society and "less than" the recognizeably human members of that society.

For instance, in the ante-bellum American South, it was not unheard-of for young African-American slaves to serve naked in their master's houses. The nakedness of the fourteen-year-old slave boy in Georgia, passing the platters at the table of the slaveholder to the delicately-bred and virginal daughters of the house, was a sign of the social relation between them: the slave had no boundaries to transgress; his nakedness was so unimportant as to be invisible to them.

When slave purchasers opened the mouths of men and women and children on the auction block and looked at their teeth, they may have been doing what the dominant explanation claimed they were doing—checking their health. But by forcing these human beings to open a body cavity in public against their will, they were also teaching them what it meant to be a slave; and, they may have hoped, teaching them also how to be slaves. They were demonstrating, unconsciously, what they needed to demonstrate in order to live at peace with their consciences: that these creatures were not really human.

By the same token, the contemporary public strip-searching and cavity-searching of prisoners is not simply an issue of hygiene and prison security—the dominant, conscious explanation. It is also acknowledged by criminologists to be a ritualized, liminal passage that indicates to the prisoner that his autonomy has been suspended along with his physical privacy. It is designed to teach someone how to be a prisoner.

The "cold mutton" moments in our lives are designed to teach women to not recognize themselves as being human—that is, equal members of the social organism in which they are playing a part—and they are designed to help men in institutions that are male-dominated fail to recognize women co-workers, students or faculty as being human. Why should one need this help? Because explaining away inequality in the face of unrelenting competence is hard. Anthropological impulse can do the work that reason fails to master. If you can strip her, symbolically if not literally, you don't need to explain why you haven't promoted her. She is not in your league. She is literally unrecognizeable.

Human beings construct human identity around the notions of honor and of privacy. Women's sexuality, of course, is treated, variously in the East and in the West, in ways that either guarantee or make it likely that they can maintain neither sexual honor nor sexual privacy. In many Muslim countries, for instance, women have no sexual honor of their own; when they dishonor "themselves," they actually are understood to be dishonoring their male relatives. As a consequence of this denial to women of a sense of sexual dignity, it is very hard for us, as part of the ground of our epistemology, to recognize women as being human, and thus entitled to the survival level of dignity necessary to the sustenance of the human spirit.

I call upon us tonight to recognize, then, two levels on which human rights should be constructed and defended. The material, political level is easy enough to see: that is the level at which there is a club over the head, a boot in the gut, a bone splintering in a killing field. We all—or, rather, most of us, in what is called the civilized world—are well able to look at that level of rights and agree that one needs, as a human being, to be able to live free of rape, of torture, of totalitarianism, of electrodes connected to skin in a damp cell.

But there is that second level—the level of consciousness. On this level, human rights are determined by whether one is permitted or denied one's physical privacy; and one's honor. On this level of consciousness, we understand that physical dignity is something that the human being needs in order not only to feel human, but to be recognized by others as being human.

We take for granted, when it comes to men, that one cannot be truly free without honor. We recognize honor being a vital component of men's sense of their own humanity. We understand, even if we don't approve, that when men see their honor besmirched—their national flags burned, their ethnic patrilineage vilified, their religious spaces desecrated—that this is grounds for violence, if not for war. The oldest and most effective militarist propaganda uses not actual physical offences, but emotional humiliations, as spurs to a population to urge it to go to war. We understand, when it comes to men and their need for dignity, that, in E. E. Cummings' words, "There is some s . . . I will not eat."

We have no such understanding yet of the relationship between women's dignity and their humanity.

The mass of literature that Amnesty had compiled for me is testimony to this cognitive problem we have as a consequence of the routine sexual humiliation of women, and the denial to them of the right to control the boundaries of privacy around their bodies. There was one frequent tautology I noticed in the wording of the pamphlets that should have sounded weird, but, weirdly, didn't: "Human rights are women's right."

The sentence was a good one: direct, declarative, even symmetrically constructed. It was good English; one should have had no trouble understanding it. Even the lettering was clear: the words were printed boldly on the cover of one pamphlet, in white against a red background, as if provided for extra proof of the content, underneath the title was a photograph of someone. This someone was tall, thin, and walking upright; she was dark-brown-skinned, and carrying a water gourd balanced atop her head.

Yes, I agreed silently as I went over the material, that looks to me to be a human being. Indeed, I felt convinced of it. And yet: throughout the pages' account of the fight that they and others who care about human rights were waging around the world, there was evidence that that tenacious impression of mine—that this creature carrying this gourd on a riverbank of what turned out to be, according to the pamphlet's flyleaf, the southern Sudan, was, in fact, nothing other than a human being—is not taken as being obvious at all.

Listen to the language: the UN Declaration on the Elimination of Violence Against Women calls for "the universal application to women of the rights and principles with regard to equality, security, liberty, integrity and dignity of all human persons." The 1993 UN World Conference held that ". . . the human rights of women and of the girl-child are an inalienable, integral and indivisible part of universal human rights."

This rhetoric strikes me as being beyond strange and beyond sad. Beyond strange, because this tortuous language is, in essence, an Orwellian countercharge to an Orwellian evasion. Beyond sad, because of where we are located in history; we are located in that point in history at which there is no excuse. For here we are, gathered together at the very end of the twentieth century, on the farthest reach of a continent that has been scorched by war after war. And ours, we can agree, is a century which, of all centuries, should surely by now—by now—have taught us that, wherever there is any qualification of the term "human" when it comes to the act of describing people, nightmares inhere.

You can hear in this rhetoric echoes that are very old—that belong by rights to another time and place; the hateful past. For this is the exact same language as that used by nineteenth-century abolitionist and suffragist literature—language that the advocates of dehumanized groups use when they have little social support. It is the rhetoric of desperation, used when one must reason not by an appeal to commonly-held recognition of rights, but rather, first, by analogy: if a man has rights, one must assert that a black slave is a man before one can argue for his rights; "Am I not a man and a brother?" asked one famous abolitionist image of an African-American slave in shackles.

The very same year that Elizabeth Cady Stanton's and Susan B. Anthony's suffrage periodical, *The Revolution*, debuted, Anthony Trollope's heroine Emily said to her sister, "It is a very poor thing to be a woman." To which Nora replied, "It is perhaps better than being a dog . . . but, of course, we can't compare ourselves to men."

Well, apparently, a hundred and twenty eight years later, we are still trying, controversially enough, to situate ourselves in a relationship to the world of rights that is distinct from that of dogs and perhaps even comparable to that of men.

Perhaps the next time a woman is symbolically made naked against her will in an institutional setting, we will understand what is going on with a deeper perception than the one that obtains now. A truly historic event took place in this regard in Beijing—women's right to sexual dignity was affirmed. For the first time ever, women were acknowledged to have the inalienable right to say no to sex that is sought against their will; that resolution carries the implication, which perhaps will take another revolution, that women have certain rights to say yes as well. Perhaps this breakthrough will herald a new time in which we enjoy a heightened sense of what rights are; and in which we understand that a person needs physical dignity—and, for the purposes of this address, a female person needs sexual dignity—just as profoundly as she needs clean water, free balloting, and freedom from the fear of jackboots clattering to the door.

5

Each Man in His Cave

Michèle le Doeuff

It has been said that of all political topics, dogs are the worst. For whatever a city council member may say on that issue, she will be the loser and irritate everyone, from people who love dogs to people who resent them, everybody feeling frustrated one way or the other. Experience proves this theory to be only too true.

Still, there is a topic which is even worse than dogs, and that is matrimony. Never discuss it in public, or do so at your own risk: this seems to have been the motto of many politicians throughout Europe since the war. The family is safe, as a topic. Just say how deeply committed you are to defending family values: some electors will be pleased, others will simply shrug their shoulders and call it empty talk, many will find the echo of so familiar a cliché reassuring. Few will wonder what you have in mind, fewer indeed will whisper unseemly words such as "incestuous rape," "molested wives and children," "clitoridectomy," "murder happening mostly amongst relatives," "women slaving to take care of the elderly, the young and males of all ages," even though some will be alert enough to read your statement as hinting that women should leave the labour market—and perhaps, after a while, others will question your personal behaviour and your family life. All in all, though, and for the time being, the family is still a tolerably safe topos, whereas marriage, the socio-legal core of the family, remains unmentionable.

For let us consider what has taken place in many European countries in our own times: on the one hand, many changes have been introduced by governments in the legal framework of matrimony; on the other hand these alterations were mostly carried out in the quietest possible way. One day, you could discover just by chance—though perhaps you did not—that, as a married woman, you could at last have a regular bank account and chequebook, whereas a year before all you could have was a joint account with your husband, or a married woman's special account.

Another day, you might read a brief article in a women's magazine about the new possibility for you to legitimize a baby who was not your husband's child, whereas previously it would have been automatically considered to be your husband's, unless the said husband himself decided to deny his paternity or unless your lover legitimized it quickly as born to him "from an unknown mother." I am not making any of this up. Another day, if you were lucky, you might hear someone mentioning that adultery does not exist in France any longer (as an offense I mean). If you were very lucky, you might even be told that, from the time of Napoleon until the previous week, France had a double definition of adultery: for a woman, it took place as soon as she had intercourse with another man, whilst for a man it was defined as giving accommodation to another woman under the marital roof.

Of course, you were never told these trivial details on your wedding day. You just listened to a speech to the effect that the husband chose the marital residence, that it was compulsory for the wife to live with him wherever he settled, and that it was compulsory for him to receive her there. In church, you got a sermon about wedded bliss and morality. Yet no one ever took the trouble to explain to you the legal obligations deriving from your taking on the status of married woman. It is still so, of course. Silence about how things stand is still de rigueur, and whenever a reform is introduced it is done secretively and with scarcely a report in the press, as if it were an administrative matter, not a political one—a dull administrative matter, just like driving test requirements.

There is one exception to this, though. When divorce was first introduced in Italy a quarter of a century ago, that at least was treated as a political question and a public debate took place. The same may apply to Ireland, where it was first introduced last year (and not a moment too soon). But how many people on the Continent knew that divorce was not a possibility in Ireland? How many of them have forgotten by now? And how many citizens here know that European governments duly acknowledge the regulations of the countries to which migrants still belong, with the result that a North African woman living in Europe may be repudiated by her husband and thereby lose all her rights in the blink of an eye, including her right to be here? It is in our name, as citizens, that laws are passed and regulations maintained. Therefore it is our responsibility to check whether they are respectful of human rights. Yet we seldom apply the demand for human rights to the so-called private sphere and, what is worse, public awareness or memory seems to find it impossible to register any particulars concerning wedlock. A non-knowledge of matrimonial law seems compulsory. Therefore, when a young woman today comes to wonder "to wed or not to wed?" (a question which is in itself a luxury, for it is not every woman who has the choice), the only thing a friend can suggest is: "go and read the law," even though one must suspect the law itself does not tell it all.

It is not just in our culture that a knowledge of the most obvious rules concerning matrimony is tacitly forbidden. Last year, an Algerian colleague gave a paper in my seminar about present situation of women in Algeria. She described the terrorist attacks on Algerian women as the serious issue they are, and explained that they need to be seen in relation to the Family Code passed and maintained by so-called legal governments. This Family Code, an equally serious issue, does not recognise women as persons in their own rights. For instance, the bride's consent is not required at her own wedding. For the ceremony or legal act to be performed, two men have to say "yes," the bridegroom and a bride's male relative. And my guest added: "I know this for sure, I have been through that ceremony; it was my brother who was asked, not I." She was implying that, in order to know, one must have been through it personally, and I believe she was right. There is a blatant cognitive discrepancy: it is very easy to know about these matters of procedure, yet except through personal and painful experience no one does, not even a senior academic, as our Algerian friend is.

A somewhat similar point was made by one of the first feminist theoreticians who ever took up the question of married life as a philosophical topic. Her name was Gabrielle Suchon. She lived in Burgundy at the end of seventeenth century, and wrote a book in favour of the single life, *Du Célibat Volontaire*.[1] There is, she said, a misappreciation or downright lack of knowledge regarding marriage, which seems to be one of the conditions enabling it to exist at all. For if people knew what married life was, they would never wed. Quoting from an author she left unnamed and who had maintained that matrimony is so full of miseries that anyone who took a close look at it might well be put off, she elaborates: "In order to understand that, one must consider married women's duties. These are so heavy that, to accomplish them, it would be necessary for wives to be adorned with as many virtues as a saint's sister." Gabrielle Suchon's method is worthy of note. After first taking up, in a general way, complaints expressed by male authors against wedded life, and without initially expressing a gendered point of view, she then substantiates the neutral statement that "married life is full of hardships" by saying that married life is a burden for women, and that therefore it is a burden period. Philosophically speaking, her method means that what is experienced by women *is*, and since absolutely speaking *it is*, it provides data and landmarks that are even capable of giving some truth to statements which, if you had just men's position in mind, would not be so very self-evident. She was not a relativist, she simply took seriously what happens to women and assumed, with some success indeed, that social life as such is more clearly analysed if you first consider what society plans for women.

Could we not take up Suchon's endeavour and inquire, after her, what a woman's point of view could reveal about in matrimony nowadays? My plain answer would be that our century believes in human rights; women are sometimes amongst the beneficiaries, but wives are the blind spot of our approach to human rights. Any definition of human rights, because it functions as a touchstone, a reference independent of (and superior to) any national legislation, is therefore a fundamental scale against which one may judge any state's policy as well as so-called customary practice. But what international organisation, what non-governmental agency, has ever campaigned for a definition of human rights as something that should be protected in the framework of matrimony?

True, something is dawning in the results of the 1995 Beijing 4th Conference on Women: paragraph 224 of the *Platform for Action* reads that "governments should take urgent action to combat and eliminate all forms of violence against women in private and public life, whether perpetrated or tolerated by the state or private persons." It is important because private life is—at last!—depicted by an international document as a sphere where women are at risk, exposed to forms of violence for which the state must be held responsible, even when it seems simply to tolerate them. Furthermore, this document is important because it considers every form of violence as being destructive of women's dignity and fundamental rights. Let my radical friends *not* call it insufficient, and let my optimistic friends *not* assume that now the field is won: such a statement is just a beginning. If we really want to see this new hope mature, we must take it up, further it, and for instance examine our human rights culture to see where and how it still fails to protect women, especially women who are wives.

The Beijing text is a "platform,"—not a legal text that could be enforced, and for the time being, I do not know of any global declaration of human rights that broaches the topic of rights within matrimony. But I do know of just the opposite, namely a declaration of human rights giving permission to states to rule however they wish in the sphere of family life. In 1950 in Rome, a European Convention for the Protection of Human Rights and Fundamental Freedoms was adopted by a few countries; later on, other countries joined in, one by one, as soon as they could meet the requirements. Moreover, some additions to the text have been made. This Convention created the European Court of Human Rights, and it nowadays covers a broader Europe than the EEC or the Maastricht European Community. But the Maastricht Treaty being based on it, we may say it is the oldest *and* the most recent European text, as well as geographically the widest. Two articles in it, which may look benign, are, if carefully examined, simply frightening: article 8 reads: "Everyone has a right to respect for his private and family life, his home and his correspondence"; and article 12 reads "Men and women of marriageable age have the right to marry and to found a family, according to the national laws governing the exercise of this right."

This means that nations have an absolute right to legislate about marriage and the family. May a state rule out divorce and still meet the demands of this convention? Yes. May a state rule out all kinds of family planning, and even information about contraception or abortion, and still meet the demands of the European Convention? Yes again, since Ireland ratified this declaration in 1966, and France as early as 1950, at the same time as Germany and Greece. But why refer to the 1950s, when such a text could also have suited the ideological needs of fascist Italy or Nazi Germany a few years before? It stipulates merely that national laws regulate matrimony and the family, with the result that a government could forbid some types of marriages or introduce forced sterilization, without being at odds with this article. This 1950 article should have been deemed obsolete after the impressive women's movements that developed since then. But far from being outdated, it was reproclaimed a few years ago, as the moral and political foundation of the Maastricht European Community. True, an addition had been made in 1984, stating that "spouses shall enjoy equality of rights and responsibility of a private law character between themselves, and in their relations with their children," a valuable addition, certainly. Still, it does not preclude that states may do whatever they want about reproductive rights and divorce, just as states may also fail to interfere with domestic violence. The article about "the right to respect for his family life and home" rings like Dickens' remark that "a man may call his house an island if he likes."[2] Now the legislator elaborates: "there shall be no interference with the exercise of this right except such as is in accordance with the law." Which law? And what if the law does not want to interfere and rescue battered wives? True, there is something about interference in the interest of health and morality, and on this we may work, to demand a more explicit paragraph or a brand new article about the protection of women's and children's human rights within the family. And we must do that, with reference to the Beijing Platform. Otherwise, the right of national legislations will remain the major right acknowledged, if not the only one. And when a discretionary power of the state is asserted, a blatant totalitarian framework is laid down. The one original feature of this framework is that it encases—like a box within a box—a family home in the state, like a state within the state, with the state's unreserved approval.

So this is what they think in Europe about matrimony and the production of children, namely that these matters fall within the competence of nations or states, and have little to do with human rights. They think like this at the end of the twentieth century, but this may be a remote outcome of a debate started in Ancient Greece. For let us turn to a seminal passage in Homer, in which the poet describes the Cyclopes' way of life.[3] The Cyclopes have no political organisation, he says, no assembly to discuss things, but each man, in his own vaulted cave, rules over his wives and children. That passage has been quoted by both Plato and Aristotle, as describing a savage state of nature. Plato claimed that customs like that, however primitive, are in themselves already a certain kind of political organisation, whereas Aristotle regretted that in many cities legislators still neglected to rule on family matters, thus allowing every man to please himself and live like a Cyclopes. Both certainly thought that a state regulation of family matters would be superior to that situation, and formal law better than this traditional way of life which, in Plato's words, is already a political organisation. Aristotle even claimed that, society being *the* whole and the family just a part of that whole, society or the state come first. None of them, of course, had women's or children's human rights in mind; they simply thought it would be in the interest of the state itself to be somehow the ruler in this family cave.

Yet their account implies that patriarchy exists in the state of nature as well as through traditions and state-regulated laws, and in pretty much the same way. In a sense, these male authors could imagine that their patriarchal power was supported by nature, tradition and the state at the same time. How secure in their position they must have felt if everything conspired to fasten their grip on wives and children! More recent male philosophers have taken up such a view. In Sir Thomas More's description of the Utopian family, husbands of course chastise wives, and this is described as a local custom which is in conformity with the natural order and guaranteed by the Republic. Sir Thomas More is crucial reading for us today. On the one hand, he tried to suggest an equality of a sort between women and men, as far as work, leisure, access to learning, and perhaps politics were concerned. But some equality between women and men did not imply the abolition of husbands' authority over their wives. Even though wives are women, and many women wives, a wife is not a woman: these are two different concepts, though the same human being, one in the flesh, may be both. Therefore, at a political level, you can have a system in which women and men have more or less equal rights, but in which wives are subjected to their husbands. Reading Sir Thomas More today may give us a warning: campaigning for equality between women and men, that is to say between human beings seen as independent one from the other, is just a part of our agenda—a small part, perhaps, if matrimony is still compulsory and if, through matrimony, a bride is given away to a man to whom she will be subjugated. After all, the Algerian Constitution has it that women and men are equal, and the Israeli Constitution reads the same; but then through the Family Code in Algeria and through religious regulation of the family in Israel, the sex-equality principle is simply overturned. And in the view of many people, it is not the rights of women which determine the rights of wives, it is the position of wives which restricts the definition of women's rights. Last month in Berne, and in a women's conference, an elderly justice of the peace denied that contraception was a woman's right, because, she explained, "the husband must have his say, and if they can't agree on the matter, the situation is serious and may lead to a divorce." Not a woman's right, because not a wife's right, says a woman—no wonder the Beijing Platform *of Action* merely reaffirmed "that reproductive rights rest on the recognition of the basic right of all couples and individuals to decide freely, etc."[4] I'm told that with the Vatican represented in Beijing and actively organizing other fundamentalist countries, it was already an achievement to have this paragraph at all in the Platform. However, one must hear a slippery compromise in it: reproductive rights are said to be couples' and individuals' rights, not women's rights, with the result that men are very present in the wording.

It is not every male philosopher who, while stating that wives are subjected to their husbands, has nonetheless tried like Sir Thomas More to imagine a kind of equality between women and men. My point is rather that male philosophers have mostly taken the subjection of wives for granted, and granted by nature, tradition, and law. If you read together Rousseau's *Émile*, *Lettre à d'Alembert* and *Nouvelle Héloïse*, you will see that our enlightened Jean-Jacques draws on the same pattern: patriarchal marriage comes from necessity, from nature (oh, surely not from the state of nature? Well, at least from "the order of Nature God has established"[5]) and also from tradition. A self-respecting state, namely Geneva, guarantees it in full. Now, when one has named Sir Thomas More and Rousseau, one has mentioned authors supposed to be amongst the most imaginative philosophers. If *even they* upheld a classical patriarchal view on marriage, the topic must be hopeless. Perhaps it is just as in Raymond Briggs' cartoon *Fungus The Bogeyman*, which describes a world where people appreciate rotten eggs and wet sheets, where they do not want to catch a "hot," where graffiti on the walls record sayings of wisdom, a totally different world—but the husband, served by his wife, grumbles about the food she has cooked, while also scolding the children for having disgustingly clean nails. The cartoonist described an upside-down world but could not imagine different relations in a household. And male philosophers, however daring they may prove in other respects, found it impossible to conceive of a couple without some male power in it.

True, there has been a bit of a debate, from John Locke onward. Some have wondered whether marriage is a contract or not, and the modern idea of divorce derives from this debate. Kant thought it was a contract, and Hegel called Kant's theory shameful. Never mind: they all agreed that, as long as a marriage lasted, "the rule *naturally* falls to the man's share" (to quote John Locke, an author sometimes praised by contemporary commentators for having invented "companionable marriage"). And, true again, on his wedding day, John Stuart Mill promised never to use the powers conferred on him by the law of marriage, and to respect Harriet Taylor's freedom "as if no such marriage had taken place."[6] Mill's statement is a superb moral "protest," but not a theory. It is as if, after centuries of patriarchal philosophy on wedlock, it was impossible for a man to produce a progressive theory: the only good thing to say about a marriage is that it has not taken place.

In this century my dear male colleagues have fallen silent on the subject, just as politicians have, leaving the floor to demographers, who note that marriage is declining everywhere in Europe, and to ethnographers, who produce wonderful diagrams showing complex systems in which women are exchanged by men. Sometimes they raise (after Margaret Mead, I think) one point of interest: namely, terms of kinship cannot be translated from a given language or culture into a different one. It is never safe, for example, to translate any foreign term by "granny" or "uncle." But there is one exception: "wife of" can safely be translated from any language to any other one. Is there a universal position for a woman who is somebody's wife, then? Could we really suggest there is a common feature in the social definition of wedlock, whatever the culture, and even when we are aware that, in the same given country, there may be very different forms of marriages? Let me draw a parallel between a study by Georges Dumézil and one by Bridget Hill, in order to show that multiplicity or difference may be more apparent than real.

Georges Dumézil's book on Indo-European marriages offers a complex picture.[7] In Ancient India, he says, there was not just one form of marriage, but eight, though some documents mention only five or six. In very Ancient Rome, there were three different modes of giving a bride away, one solemn and for free, one by selling the bride to the husband-to-be, and one through *usus* (if a woman stayed a whole year with the man to whom her father had given her). There was a fourth form which the Romans considered as having existed in legendary times only, namely the acquisition of a woman by violent abduction followed by the taming of the bride, the relationship being eventually made stable by the passing of time. The rape of the Sabine women is, of course, *the* example of that. This mode is also listed in Indian Catalogues, with details: it takes place when a man "after killing or injuring [opponents] breaks into a dwelling and abducts a maiden who cries out and weeps." A document quoted by Dumézil notes that wise men think highly of this way of marrying, for it makes the very best wives. This mode of marrying seems to evoke warfare situations and it could substantiate a view upheld by Anderson and Zinsser, that "in early warrior cultures, the men of a defeated group were slaughtered and the women enslaved."[8] As concubines and servants, the two feminist historians say, but in the light of Dumézil's work I should like to add sometimes also as wives.

If we now jump abruptly from these ancient times to eighteenth-century England, and leave Dumézil for Bridget Hill, we are going to discover an equally complex picture.[9] Confusion between betrothal and wedding; overlapping of three jurisdictions, namely the Church, the state, and custom enforced by the local community; marriage with or without parental consent; clandestine marriages of all sorts, broomstick weddings, problems of grammar, with confusion of tenses (so that a woman who could not clearly distinguish between "I will" and "I shall" might find herself married unawares); with some forms of marriage, women being able to claim a dowry and with other forms not; a lot of people disagreeing about what was a "regular marriage," squires and matrons trying to promote formal marriage in Church; etc., etc. A remarkable chaos.

If marriage, in the same spot and time, may take so many different forms, if indeed this very multiplicity is a feature of at least the Indo-European heritage, what is it then that makes a marriage a marriage? Have these different forms something in common? Yes, they have: whatever the mode, the woman comes under a man's authority and hand, and there is something identifiable as marital authority. If you see marriage as a deal between a woman's male relatives and a man, of course there are different forms; but when you look at the result for the woman, it is pretty much the same: she is submitted to a husband. In legal Franco-English jargon, she becomes a *feme covert*, and marriage deprives her of any legal existence. In Rome, she became a *filia* in the husband's family. True, Dumézil claimed that there was one form of marriage which was without authority, or rather without a transfer of paternal authority to the husband. His theory was based on a no longer accepted reading of an inscription, according to which a girl's tutors promised the husband that: "If she does not comply with you, it will be our duty, by means of our tutelage, to restore the peace." Would a quick feminist comment on Dumézil's construction be out of place? However unsound it may be, it was based on the possibly right assumption that, in Ancient Rome, and perhaps later on, a man would never take a woman as a spouse unless his domination over her was formally guaranteed by some social agency or other, either the free hand over her that society guaranteed him or a special pledge by her male relatives. If it takes more than a man to enforce wifely submission, if social order must come as a prop, so much for nature as an adequate basis of marital power. Even marriage by abduction and the enslaving of a woman from a defeated group was bound to find support within the man's group. And in England common law marriage was enforced by the local community.

Since I have drawn a parallel between Hill's and Dumézil's works, I must also emphasize a contrast. In Dumézil's book, it is always hinted that there never was much to worry about. Surely the father consulted a girl before marrying her off, surely *pakari* did not mean to pacify a rebel like *pacare* in Ciceronian Latin, but just some influence on the woman's mood.[10] And, when discussing forms of marriage, he insists that they were based on the woman's autonomy, thus betraying the not-so-highly demanding definition of autonomy he applied where women were concerned. The same with my distinguished colleague Jean Bottéro: of course the Mesopotamian family was completely patriarchal and women were owned by husbands just like the house, ox, and plough; but in Mesopotamia as everywhere else, it rested with every woman's personality and energy to make herself respected by her husband.[11] But Bridget Hill is constantly worried, she is certain that in eighteenth century England some girls were married without even knowing they were getting married; she is certain horrible things took place, such as wife-selling. She fully describes the sort of power a man, by marrying, acquired over a woman. So let me recommend a comparison of these books to anyone interested in the effects of gender on academic research, since the realities they describe are quite similar, but the undertones and implications of the description are so very different.

Perhaps now we should turn to situations where marriage declines or hardly exists in order better to understand, by a negative analysis, what it is when it is. In the seventies, when campaigning for reproductive rights in France, we also exposed the dreadful conditions of life in homes where, before and after giving birth, single women were sheltered, that is to say withdrawn from public view, like eyesores. Because of that, the French Republic created a subsidy for "isolated parents," a term referring in fact to single abandoned mothers. They took this step in order to show that there was an alternative to abortion and also to salvage a high birthrate. However conservative the reasons, this subsidy has helped many a single woman who is not well-off to continue a pregnancy and have the child she wants. As usual, this new possibility was not much discussed in France, either before the bill was passed or even after the fact, except in the French West Indies. There you could hear some men complaining about it, surprisingly enough, since marriage was never popular, not even common law marriage, in Martinique and Guadeloupe, from the time of slavery onward. Promiscuity, or a precarious partnership men felt free to break whenever they wanted, had always been the norm. As a result, for several centuries many households were composed of an abandoned mother and her children. In the West Indies, the subsidy made a real difference for women, as it did of course in Continental France. But why did men resent it? Because, though still free to walk out on their partners, they were no longer as free to stay as they used to be. Women, not needing men's financial cooperation as much as they did before, could then take the initiative in ending the relationship. In Continental France, we were discovering that thanks to contraception and abortion we were less often forced to marry, whereas, when we had no reproductive rights, the well-known retailer "Pronuptia" sold a third of its bridal dresses with a loose waist, one wedding out of three being followed by a birth within seven months. Accidental pregnancy made many of us wed, especially when we were still too young to have a sufficient income. Birth control, which enabled us to postpone the first pregnancy, and a state subsidy for single motherhood, have indeed helped many women to get out of marrying, just as they have brought a dramatic change in the asymmetrical relationships in the West Indies. Birth control, less shabby salaries for women, and crèches could achieve the same result, and on a larger scale, as Communist East Germany seems to have proved. Looking at these recent historical experiences, we may suggest also that when women are guaranteed free access to birth control, the stigma attached to children born out of wedlock and to their mothers vanishes.

But then, what is, or was, marriage, if parameters like these can make it decline? Why did enslaved people not marry? How is it that, in apartheid South Africa, over 40 percent of children were born out of wedlock, with the figure reaching 70 percent in the Cape Town African community.[12] Sandra Burman and Eleanor Preston-Whyte, editors of a volume devoted to that problem, beg their readers not to mistake such a situation with the current phenomenon in Western countries.[13] The mistake shall not be made. On the other hand, it may throw some light on what marriage is, to consider how downright social oppression for both sexes tends to destroy marriage, just as women's liberation makes it decline as a norm. For the West Indies in the seventeenth century an important source may document the case, a Dominican missionary called Jean-Baptiste Labat having left full-length memoirs.[14] He drew a contrast between French and English slave-owners. The French, who tried to press the slaves into Christianity, also insisted that Africans observed matrimony, a demand which was not necessary with the first generation, since recently enslaved Africans maintained their own traditions in that respect, traditions missionaries thought highly of. But the demand vastly failed with further generations, namely with people born in slavery, in spite of the use of means of coercion. So much for tradition, perhaps, if it outlives freedom for one generation only, and so much for an attempt to enforce marriage *just* by regulations and punishments. A man born in slavery was apparently not willing to marry an equally enslaved woman, even when some social pressure was exerted. Perhaps a male slave could not see the point of marrying. When a man does not own himself, how could he own a woman who already has one permanent other owner? How could he possess the children since they were also the master's property? The resistance displayed by enslaved African descendants against marrying, in spite of African traditions, French coercion and social pressure, may reveal the meaning of marriage for a male individual: it is ownership of a wife and children, and if these were owned by another man, it would be self-contradictory to own them. And let me add: even common law marriage requires a community to enforce it, and make the ownership real; slavery and apartheid clearly destroyed this requisite.

The English colonials' views were different from those of the French. To quote Labat: "The English do not spare their Blacks much. . . . They are considered virtually as cattle to whom all is permitted as long as they strictly carry out their duties. The English tolerate their having several women and their leaving these when they wish. As long as they produce many children, and work hard and are in good health, their masters are satisfied."[15] Therefore, producing many children is described as a slave's duty, mentioned even before working hard, and while the exemption from matrimony is perhaps not to be described as an overt sociotechnology designed to encourage a prolific production of children, it was at least something to be tolerated as long as it led to the production of many children. In early nineteenth-century England William Wilberforce, while exhorting the British to terminate slavery or at least to mitigate the gross injustice of it, took up the matter of the absence of marriage in the West Indies and put forward a cynical argument: it is in the interest of slave owners to promote marriage, since they want to keep up the numbers of their slaves.[16] This demi-abolitionist saw matrimony as a sociotechnology that helped lead to a higher birthrate than promiscuity, and I suspect this is also why the French tried to enforce matrimony.

The point in itself is not just based on the religious assumption that matrimony is a blessing created by God to help people carry out his command "Be fruitful and multiply." The matter is not simply mystical. There is a long Christian tradition against married women's celibacy. Let me quote a sixteenth century summary:

> Saynt Paule speketh full wysely for the admonition of good women, where he techeth the churche of god: a woman hath no power of her own body but her husband . . . saynt Augustine dothe not allow perpetual chastitie in a maried woman without her husband be content with the same. Wherfore

there is a holy man, whether it be saynt Hieronyme or some other (i wot not well) that dispreyseth one Celantyne a vertuaous woman and a good wyfe bicause she avowed perpetuall chastitee without her husbandes consent. For a woman hathe no power on her owne body, no not unto the goodness of continence.[17]

The message is unmistakable: A married woman may not say no to marital intercourse. We could add, because she may not, matrimony is likely to produce more many children than, say, free love. Outside matrimony, if a woman really feared a pregnancy, she could sometimes say no to intercourse. The tradition called "Christian" by some is not very different from an apology for rape in marriage. Therefore let me put forward a hypothesis: perhaps the interest nations take in matrimony, that is to say in a man's power over his wife, was precisely that? Perhaps communities enforce marriage, and common law marriage, because they expect to be sufficiently reproduced as communities? But then, if matrimony is aimed at turning women into sexual slaves and reproductive mares, surely a philosophy of human rights should have something to say about it?

Marital authority is—perhaps primarily—authority over the marital bed. For the husband it concerns his obtaining intercourse whenever he wants, and even if the wife does not. Correlatively, a wife is a woman on whom a man may inflict more pregnancies than she wants, with the approval of the group they both belong to. This would account for the interest nations take in maintaining matrimony and marital power, as long as birth control technology is not around, and in the hands of women, at which stage forced intercourse stops being interesting for the community. And let me make it clear: matrimony is not, in my view, so-called male violence sanctioned by law. Matrimony is a structure through which society fashions male sexuality so that it may become potentially violent or insensitive, thus transforming male libido into what appears to be a need, and not a desire, a need that must be satisfied. Men, in my view, could complain as well as we should about what matrimony has done to them, since male sexuality has been made into a *"naturally* aggressive sexuality," and the blame, when there is blame, is then put on a masculine nature (just as the praise, when praise there was, went to a so-called inherent virility). In my view, these sexual attitudes and behaviours were socially constructed by communities interested in numerous new generations, more numerous indeed than women could want or stand.

Perhaps the interest nations took or take in matrimony, that is to say in a man's power over his wife, was precisely that? I am trying here to take into account something Marx's distinguished colleague Friedrich Engels never completely explained: how is it that nations, communities or states take such an interest in matrimony and in women's oppression within the family? Engels called marriage "the historical defeat of the female sex," and blamed it all on private property, which requires legitimate heirs. We have a problem with such an explanation today: though private property and inheritance have not been abolished at all, one child out of three in many developed countries is now born out of wedlock, and with a committed father, adultery for women is no longer the crime it used to be, and marriage, perhaps every woman's defeat, seems to be declining. I believe we must turn to other ways of explaining why societies, before birth control was introduced, were so interested in marriage. *A contrario*, we must note that feminists managed to raise the issue of rape in marriage only after we had conquered reproductive rights. It was a difficult issue to raise, and our efforts to simply name it were indeed perceived as shocking. Nonetheless, in some countries at least, we succeeded in making courts acknowledge that marital intercourse without a wife's consent is rape.[18] It is my guess that, when forced intercourse was no longer liable to produce more numerous children than a woman could want, because of birth control in her hands, states lost interest in authoritarian intercourse and more or less agreed to legislate against it. Before that, by refusing to acknowledge forced marital intercourse as what it is, namely a rape, legislations, along with the Church, simply protected the practice, even guaranteed it as lawful and holy. Many examples of domestic violence are merely what not so long ago legislations acknowledged as a man's right of correction over a wife and, in many cases, wife-beating is related to forced marital intercourse. In so-called natural male violence, one must decipher the remnants of what societies encouraged a husband to do whenever his wife did not comply with him.

You surely do not want another hour-long paper on societies which would rather believe in a lower birthrate, or at least in a birthrate they could lower for a given time. You could find sociotechnologies for that described in Aristotle, a long while before Malthus. Marriage again, with a corollary demand of pre-nuptial chastity, is the traditional technique: just raise the age of consent, and it will more or less do. But if the truth must be told, I cannot name a single society which would have been really anti-natalist in the long run and for every social class. Societies always retain the option of turning back to the opposite policy in favour of a higher birthrate.

The Cyclopes' vaulted cave, in which they ruled over their wives and children, at a time when there was no assembly to discuss things, is a myth which still has to be challenged, over and over again. Such a cave never existed, as a secret enclave or a natural islet severed from assemblies where men discuss things. I doubt there ever was a society which merely tolerated men's violence against women: societies organize it, and organize also some forms of violence and repression by women against other women, to the same end. All the same, and even though the Beijing Platform fails to acknowledge women's full reproductive rights and also still assumes there is somehow a cave, with a home-baked violence towards women in it, its demand that governments take steps to eliminate all forms of violence against women, and in private life, is a highly valuable breakthrough. It is our local responsibility now to turn to the Council of Europe and insist they include in The European Convention for the Protection of Human Rights a good paragraph about measures to stop all forms of domestic violence; and we must demand that reproductive rights be recognized by the said Convention for what they are, namely one of the fundamental freedoms deserving to be stated and guaranteed. And, if I am right when suggesting that, in the hands of women, these rights also produce a historical mutation apt to uncover in retrospect and *a contrario* the structure of many forms of violence towards women, perhaps then, before thanking my patient audience, I may also take the opportunity of begging Amnesty International to consider the addition of a sixteenth step to the already valuable list entitled Amnesty International's Fifteen Steps to Protect Women's Human Rights. It could read "Reproductive rights are women's rights and women's rights are human rights."

Notes

I should like to thank Saba Bahar and Claude Barbey-Morand, who prompted this stream of thought through their questions and objections in my seminar, René Amacker, who spared me a blunder, and Valerie Fehlbaum, who was the friendly reader of successive drafts.

1. Gabrielle Suchon, *Du Célibat Volontaire ou la Vie Sans engagement*, 2 vols. (Paris: J. et M. Guignard, 1700). Available in microfilm from Bibliothèque Nationale in Paris. Chapters of this book were edited by Séverine Auggret (Paris: Indiga & Côté-femmes, 1994).

2. Charles Dickens, *Nicholas Nickeleby*, chap. 7.

3. Homer *Odyssey* 9.114ff.; Plato *Laws* 3.680b; Aristotle *Nicomachean Ethics* 10.10.1180a25 and *Politics* 1.2.1252b20.

4. Paragraph 223.

5. Rousseau, *La Nouvelle Héloïse*, IIIe partie, chap. 18, pléïade, p. 357.

6. Ann P. Robson and John M. Robson, eds., *Sexual Equality: Writings by John Stuart Mill, Harriet Taylor Mill, and Helen Taylor* (Toronto: University of Toronto Press, 1994), pp. 47–48.

7. George Dumézil, *Mariages Indo-Européens* (Paris: Éditions Payot, 1979).

8. Bonnie S. Anderson and Judith P. Zinsser, *A History of Their Own: Women in Europe from Prehistory to the Present* (Harmondsworth, U.K.: Penguin, 1988), 1:21.

9. Bridget Hill, *Women, Work, and Sexual Politics in Eighteenth Century England* (Oxford: Basil Blackwell, 1989).

10. Dumézil, *Mariages Indo-Européens* , pp. 99, 57.

11. Jean Bottéro, *Babylone et la Bible: Entretiens avec Hélène Monsacré* (Paris: Les Belles-Lettres, 1994), pp. 198–199.

12. Sandra Burman and Eleanor Preston-Whyte, eds., *Questionable Issue: Illegitimacy in South Africa* (Oxford: Oxford University Press, 1992), p. xiv.

13. Burman and Preston-Whyte, *Questionable Issue*, p. xv.

14. Jean Baptist Labat, *Nouveau Voyage aux Isles de l'Amérique*, 8 vols. (1722–1742; reprint, Paris: Ed. du Père Labat [reproduction photomécanique], 1992).

15. Labat, *Nouveau Voyage aux Isles de l'Amérique*, 4:401.

16. William Wilberforce, *An Appeal to the Religion, Justice, and Humanity of the Inhabitants of the British Empire, in Behalf of the Negro Slaves in the West Indies* (London: J. Hatchard and Son, 1823), p. 15. I am greatly indebted to Saba Bahar for this reference.

17. Vivès, *De Institutione Faeminae Christianae* (Anvers, 1524). I am quoting from the early and frequently reprinted English translation by Richard Hyrde, *A Very Fruteful and Pleasant Boke callyd the Instruction of a Christen Woman* (London: T. Berth, 1541), p. 66. See also p. 80. The initial reference to St. Paul is in 1 Corinthians 7.

18. In Switzerland, a group of women lawyers succeeded, after a pretty long struggle, in making legislation acknowledge the concept. Moreover, they produced a theoretical essay entitled "What Do We Mean by Rape?" extant in typescript: Barbara Fischer, Elisabeth Freivogel, Suzanne Sprecher-Bertschi, Lisa Stärkle, et l'Association Femmes-Juristes-Démocrates, "Qu'entendons-nous par viol? Les délits sexuels d'un point de vue féministe" (Basel: Bâle, 1988). I am greatly indebted to Claude Barbey-Morand for giving me a photocopy.

6

Women's Rights in Today's Political Climate

Shere Hite
with responses by Alison Jeffries and Sarah Ansari

Shere Hite's lecture, although not written for this purpose, forms an excellent closing piece for this volume. It raises many of the same questions as the other pieces, but crosses the boundaries between liberalism and difference feminism, and between liberal and radical feminist responses to the problems identified. As such it focuses our minds on the underlying debates in feminism and political theory that are reflected and developed in the six lectures. This process is facilitated by the style of the lecture, which was presented as a series of questions posed to the audience.

It seemed, therefore, that we could best do justice to the Socratic style of Shere Hite's delivery, and at the same time bind together the themes of this volume, by using her lecture as part of a dialogue. Consequently, we have presented this paper in sections interspersed with our own responses. These comments reflect on the significance of the points raised by Hite in the context both of the themes of this volume and of some of the broader debates in contemporary feminist analysis.

The Invisible War

We are witnessing one of the biggest assaults on rationalism, tolerance and the secular tradition of human rights in three centuries.

It is mostly an assault aimed at women, women are on the firing line of this global conflict. Women's rights are at stake, more than anything else.

Nevertheless, women are "invisible" in the political debates on these conflicts. Just as women have always been "invisible," so today the war against women, who had begun to be visible and to speak out, is seen not as a war against women, but as a "religious revival," or "a new nationalism," "racial solidarity" and so on.

Will the democratic tradition, separation of church and state promising equal rights for all citizens, be able to withstand this attack? Will people of good will overcome centuries of the trivialisation and invisibilising of women's situation, which means that they are now conditioned not to "see" the war against women taking place?

Certainly, the plight of women in many countries seems invisible to most governments, who rarely or never include human rights abuses of women in their foreign policy. When lately has one government reprimanded another for treating "its women" badly?

The new global war is carried on by internationally connected groups of "religious" organizations, whose money is not taxed. Its emotional strength comes from the frustration of men and boys who have been treated unjustly, discriminated against, and who (sometimes) sincerely believe that "getting women back into the home" will "put things right again," that "this is what is wrong with the modern world, it has no values." They are desperate to feel powerful (again, in the case of the U.S.), and "putting the family in order" sounds like it will give them that power, at least over women.

Some of the strongest fundamentalist groups are in Iran, Saudi Arabia, the Christian coalition movement in the United States (Protestant fundamentalism), the Black Muslim movement in the United States, and in the current pope's leadership of the Vatican.

This new politics has no name. Politics-as-usual continue to be discussed in the almost-meaningless categories of "left" and "right"—though issues of sexual politics are now overwhelming these old categories. What the media may call "single issues," such as ecology and women's rights (abortion rights, domestic violence, politicians' private comportment toward women), are forming a new political spectrum. The war against women, and women's resistance, is in a way a new "cold war," and it is not likely to go away anytime soon.

The ideological attack used to justify and cover up the brutal repression of women is that "Western secularism" (democracy) is lacking spiritual profundity. This is an argument many in the West find makes them vulnerable because of an entire century of defensiveness in the face of partially justifiable "Marxist" accusations of commercialism, soulessness, and so on—stereotypes in Russia about "foreign lands" (not being as spiritual as mother Russia) which go back centuries.

It is not true that Western secularism is a-spiritual, lacking in depth, soulless. The goal of equality for all its members, even if not reached, drowned out by advertising and commercial media, is still the most spiritual, most idealistic goal around. Trying to make a "heaven" on earth.

Foreign Policy Fears of Taking "Women's Issues" Seriously

Attacks on women by supposedly religious groups all over the world are going unchallenged by the world's governments. Why did President Clinton feel justified in complaining of Iran's terrorism, but not of its genocidal policies toward over half of its population, i.e. women? The United States (and other countries) years ago should have begun a trade embargo to protest this attack on women's human rights. Now, couldn't Clinton have at least mentioned Iran's unjust targeting of women along with his other reasons for boycotting trade with Iran? Did he think to do so would be politically incorrect or unpopular, or did he just not think of it at all?

To give another example, of the averted eye stance. No government in the world has protested against the Vatican's increasing attacks of women. Why? The Vatican is sponsoring appointments of new bishops and cardinals around the world of the most reactionary fundamentalist mentality, bankrolling their newsletters and other political activities, which mainly target women, most visibly vis-à-vis abortion clinics, but which also campaign actively for certain politicians to be elected. Should governments stand by passively and allow the Catholic Church—or fundamentalist Islamic or Protestant groups—to engage in political activities in the name of "religion?" Tax free?

Yet as a result of the confusion over whether "women's rights" are a political or "private" religious issue, the foreign policy of most Western countries does not yet include the situation of women as part of a country's "human rights" record. The international community subjected South Africa to an economic embargo for its notorious policy of apartheid. But it is unthinkable that similar action would be taken against Islamic countries which treat women no better or worse than whites treated blacks in South Africa. Why isn't the press making this comparison? Why is no government on earth talking about breaking off diplomatic relations because of these attacks?

There is a strange silence and discomfort surrounding the whole issue of "women's rights," or "the woman question." This is why most politicians are unclear and do not address the questions directly; strangely, politicians who are anti "women's rights" find it easier to speak out about this than do politicians who seem to be pro women's rights. But why is this? Why is it so politically unpopular to stand up for women? Do male heads of governments feel like wimps if they do this? They would be courageous if they would take a stand.

I feel confused and I wonder how much world leaders understand about how what is going on affects women's rights and lives. It is difficult to assess from the little information one has. Do democratic politicians realize consciously the disastrous meaning of their foreign policy blindness for women? I often wonder what to make of their actions, and hope against hope that somehow some public officials will understand, get the idea, and "do something." This seems like the impossible dream.

The reason "the woman question" remains so troubled and unresolved, for politicians from John Adams (U.S. founder) up through Karl Marx and on to John Major, is because democracy promises equality, and yet women have had to struggle for over two centuries trying to get it. Many men are being dishonest about their supposed support for "democracy" when they have power and do nothing to make women's power, in government and out, equal.

Interestingly, fundamentalist groups often attack the wives of men they would like to weaken; fundamentalists in Algeria have targeted the wives of prominent politicians in late 1995; in the United States, Newt Gingrich's mother said on television that her son (the new head of the Republican Congress) thought Hilary Clinton, the president's wife, was a "bitch." This led to other attacks on her, until finally President Clinton had to come out and make a statement defending her and saying he thought she was an excellent wife and had no intention of splitting up with her. Such attacks are despicable and play on centuries-old prejudice against women, scapegoating them as the "evil ones." Elsewhere men show less awareness. Mitterand was an excellent leader of France, but like many men on the left, including some of its youngest members, he had a blind spot where women's equality was concerned, he could not integrate sex and politics. He couldn't see the future.

Governments' silent aversion of the eyes to "religious matters" such as women's status affects men's lives and well-being too. As an attorney in Barcelona told me recently, "I no longer feel free to tell my clients I am not religious, or to express openly my other opinions about things. The atmosphere is that if I don't have the right opinions, I will lose clients." We will all lose if the growing atmosphere of "religious" fundamentalism goes unchallenged. Democracy was built to insure freedom from religious persecution; it does not know how to defend itself when religion begins to persecute democracy.

The pope's 1995 announcement in the eleventh encyclical that "moral law" should take precedence over the laws of parliamentary, secular democracies was shocking. Does he mean by this to incite believers to cease obeying the laws of their governments? To rebel? He seems to want to reinstitute religious government, as his fundamentalist Islamic allies (an alliance made public at the UN Conference on World Population in Cairo in September 1994, and in Beijing in 1995) have already done in countries such as Saudi Arabia and Iran.

I have heard it said that the ongoing conflict in Bosnia is "the greatest collective failure of the West since 1938." That seems blind to me, though in part true. The West's inaction and seeming acceptance of the attacks on women and secular democracy, in both West and East, may turn out in the long run to be our greatest failure.

France and Algeria alone among nations have "seen the future" vis-à-vis these questions. In Algeria, a democratic government voted to suspend democracy in favor of a temporary military government when elections began to indicate that those elected would dismantle democracy in favour of an Islamic fundamentalist state. France and Algeria have taken public stands in favour of women's rights, and shown their intention to protect women and secular democracy from fundamentalism; sophisticated discussion is going on there about whether "extremists" (or those against the plural opinion of democracy) should be allowed to split democratic politics, end democracy, should they take power, in fact. Should a democratic government allow those to take power who would (through the rhetoric of "family values" and "moral values') end or weaken democracy? Other countries seem not yet to understand these political realities.

Response, Alison Jeffries and Sarah Ansari

In this first section of her lecture Hite draws on many of the themes raised throughout the lecture series. We are asked why women are so invisible and at the same time are reminded that this cannot be because of women's insignificance. Although the rights of women have been frequently sidelined by both national governments and the United Nations, it is also the case, as Hite provocatively suggests, that the legislative and social control of women seems to be at the heart of the politics of national renewal in both the Christian and Islamic world.

The deliberately, almost naively, simple question of why western foreign policy, which in the cold war years used the rhetoric of "human rights" so freely, seems blind to the question of women's rights has received much academic treatment. It is a theme that several of the lectures returned to. Naomi Wolf expressed herself bewildered by the tautology of the assertion that "women's rights are human rights," Marilyn French reflected on the consistent tendency to portray women as less than fully human and so undeserving of equal rights, while Martha Nussbaum argued for the power of liberal theory to incorporate the demands of women into the framework of rights.

One clearly possible explanation proposed by Hite is the dominance of men in decision making. Just as le Deouff suggests that the experience of a married woman cannot be imagined, it has to be lived, so Hite reflects on the impossibility of men making the imaginative leap necessary to cause them to focus on the consequences for women of the policies that they make. It is interesting that several commentators have noted both that the absence of women in the U.N. perhaps accounted for the inadequacies of its attempts to enforce documents such as CEDAW,[1] and that the "infiltration" of particularly U.S. feminist arguments at the highest levels was a necessary part of the change in the rhetoric and the policies of the United Nations.[2]

Yet Hite is also saying more, is she not? As she considers the relationship between men in power and the "woman question," she makes the interesting connection with their own private attitudes and responses, so breaching the liberal dam between the public and private spheres. It is not simply that male political leaders do not succeed in making policy in an adequately general way, but that they live out the relationship between the sexes in their own private lives. The possibility is tantalizingly raised that women will never get "justice" in the public realm until the private realm is itself reordered. Is this perhaps why, as Hite notes, wives of political leaders, particularly those considered Liberal, are so often attacked by conservative ("fundamentalist") opponents?

By raising the issue of the relationship between public and private, Hite also leads us directly to another widely canvassed explanation of the absence of concern for women's rights in international affairs. This is the claim that government and U.N. policy makers have tended to take too narrow a view of the scope of rights. Because of the current distribution of power in most contemporary societies, women's lives are disproportionately located in the private sphere in which liberalism is loath to intervene. Martha Nussbaum has persuasively argued in this volume that this is to restrict the scope of liberalism too far, and reflects an inadequate conceptualization of the relationship between individual and state.[3] However, those whose role it was to enforce and protect human rights tended, until very recently, to take the view that human rights are to do with what the state does, legally, while many of the violations of women's rights took place in the private sphere—or at least outside the sphere of official government action.[4] Some of the issues of greatest concern to the world's women, such as rape (including "political" rape), and violence against women in general, fell outside the scope of human rights and so was not addressed in the assessment of the human rights records of states. This has changed a great deal in the last few years. UNICEF's Progress of Nations 1997 report, for example, included a specific section on "violence against women."[5] As Michèle Le Doeuff notes with respect to aspects of the Beijing document, this move into the private sphere should not be belittled.

At the heart of this section of the lecture is Hite's clear identification of a further and more insidious source of the down-grading of women's rights. This rests on the appeal to cultural relativism: western states and international organizations have no right, it is claimed, to intervene in areas that are matter of cultural, and especially religious, tradition. Hite's forceful attack on the legitimacy of grounding policies that undermine the status of women in appeals to cultural autonomy might be best read as part of a strident renunciation of western political priorities as much as a critique of the practices of Islamic societies. Views of the non-western world and of the validity of cross-cultural commentary have evolved through a period of intense mealy-mouthed acceptance of any claim of religious or cultural particularity,[6] through to its opposite—a vigorous, although not wholly unproblematic, restatement of the universal applicability of basic principles of equality and human rights. The powerful arguments and challenges raised by Hite form part of this response. These arguments are developed at greater length below, and we will respond to some of the interesting dilemmas raised by claims of cultural specificity at that point.

Attacks on the Rights of Women: Why Are They Not Covered in the News?

Press coverage of these attacks on women and democratic states are also covered in a semi-sleeping style. Algeria, Chechnya, Afghanistan, Turkey, Pakistan—there is a serious flaw in news coverage of separatist fighting in these countries. For example, in reports of Chechnya, scene of the current fighting in Russia, a central point is left out: what are the Chechins fighting for?

Of course, they are fighting for "independence" and "their rights," but what kind of state would they install if they were to take power? Nowhere, in all the reams of coverage, is there anything about what they stand for. Instead these conflicts are reported à la Freud as if they were "young rebel" challenges to Big Daddy (for example, Russia), heroic declarations of independence—sort of fun, in fact. Beyond "fighting the tyrant" for their "independence," there is little or no information related to what kind of regime they would put into place.

Unfortunately, today, Arab pride in countries such as Palestine and Algeria is deeply entwined with Islamic fundamentalism: Observing traditionalist Islamic religious customs means you support the revolutionary struggle for independence and dignity. People can feel they "betray the cause" of national pride if they do not observe Islamic fundamentalist practices. Women are required to oppress themselves to prove their solidarity. Although fundamentalist Islam can mean either a political movement for national independence or a reactionary movement within the religion of Islam, in practice today, the two are often combined. This alliance escalates the support for fundamentalism.

In Algeria, more than 300 women have been killed for the "crime" of being "un-Islamic." The Association of Algerian women in France reports that these killings are preceded by the rape of the woman. Why? Because in order for the Islamic believer who is going to kill her to go to heaven, the woman cannot be a virgin (literally), she must be married. The latest murder described to me involved several armed men coming into a family dinner and dragging the daughter out, taking her away, raping and "marrying" her, then beheading her.

Perhaps some reporters have avoided the topic of the "religious" laws against women out of fear of being accused of religious bias. However, these are political and not religious matters. Even if a state is religious (not a secular or parliamentary democracy), this does not mean its politics do not vary and should not be discussed. Iraq, for example, treats women differently than Saudi Arabia and Iran. How women are treated under any given regime is a political, human rights issue, not a religious matter.

Reporters do not routinely take into account consequences for women of any given "revolution." If men's rights were at stake, would it be different? Consider if men were going to be put into black dresses from head to toe, on penalty of death come the "revolution" (as in Iran), I suppose there would be masses of ink spilled on the subject. The tenets of the potential new regime would become a major foreign policy issue for the world's governments.

Or if men were told that after the new regime took power, they could not drive a car, and would be punished if they tried, in fact, that they could get the death penalty if they did not cover their heads and bodies completely, would they then report clearly, "Today, Islamic fighters, who want to institute a religious state which would ban all men from public positions and force them on pain of death to wear black all over their bodies, took the town of x?"

Lumping all revolutionaries together, as "rebel heroes and tough guys," without looking into their politics, betrays a naive romanticism, a clichéd view of male heroism.

Scanty reporting of these issues was also the case with the Bosnia-Serbia conflict, few newscasters explaining the issues relating to the treatment of women—with the "trendy" exception of rape by soldiers. The reporting of Afghanistan and the "Mujahadin" showed the same sloppy tendency: the rebels were mediatized as "heroic freedom fighters," but they turned out, once in power, to impose violent, repressive laws and military hit squads on women and the entire population. A recent Amnesty report stated that four fifths of the population (including children) have been tortured or raped by roving squads.

It may be touching to present photos of elderly women in rags standing amidst bombed ruins in Bosnia or Chechnya. This is certainly a terrible reality. But such pictures seem to illustrate the story, "Isn't war terrible?," rather than to tell anything specific about the fact that it is women's bodies that are on the front-lines in these "religious" wars, it is women's rights and women's lives which are at stake.

In honesty, I find it mind-boggling and outrageous that nowhere are women's rights and the possible killing and imprisonment of millions of women by government policy so much as mentioned in all the reams of isn't-war-thrilling coverage.

Response

The blindness of the press to the suffering of women, and to attacks on women, referred to by Hite, reflects more than a simple misogyny on the part of reporters. Once again, it shows a failure of imagination and empathy which is only partly redressed by the more recent press focus on the very dramatic and visible rescinding of women's rights when the Taliban seized control of Afghanistan's capital, Kabul, during 1997.

Hite's demand to know whether the regulation of dress and behaviour would be treated as so incidental if it were men who would be affected by the rules is effective in pointing up the partiality of news values. It is fascinating to reflect that this rhetorical device echoes the Muslim Bengali writer, Rokeya Sakhawat Hossain's 1905 fantasy of reverse purdah, "Sultana's Dream."[7] Hossain has been described as an "Islamic feminist" so reinforcing the point made by Hite herself, that Islamic doctrine does not translate directly into any particular political order any more than do the doctrines of Christianity.[8]

Ironically on this point the term "fundamentalist," although widely used, can in itself obscure more than it reveals. The Islamist parties and governments of countries such as Iran, Algeria or Afghanistan could only exist in the political conditions of the twentieth century. In many ways they differ radically from "traditional" Islamic authorities of the past in the role accorded to the state, which goes far beyond the provision of conditions under which individual Muslims are enabled to live "a Godly life." They differ also from conservative Islamic Governments such as that of Saudi Arabia. Elsewhere, while Iraq is a secular state, the doctrines of Islam have on occasion been manipulated by the Ba'ath party to identify the Government with "Godliness," just as, for example, Ronald Reagan attempted to identify the Republican Party with a version of fundamentalist Protestant Christianity.

The language of the western press tends to reduce Islamic societies to stereotypes, and ironically, many Islamist leaders have been able to manipulate those stereotypes to the detriment of women. A nation such as Iran was portrayed by its own leaders as monolithic; to question the role of women within that society was to attack the cultural and national integrity of the state. By playing on the ignorance and cultural blindness of western politicians, leaders in some parts of the Islamic world have been able to obscure political actions with respect to the removal of many rights from women in religious terms. To challenge the record of such states on women's rights, therefore, could come to be portrayed as cultural imperialism. These arguments have been powerful and successful. CEDAW, for example, was the only U.N. document on human rights that allowed widespread reservation clauses, justified by the need to respect cultural norms. In consequence, several states which had legal codes at clear variance with the intentions of the document were able to ratify the convention without altering domestic legislation at all.

However, such an approach has clearly distorted much about the political and religious arguments within Islamist states and continues to do so. Women, and some men, within these states have argued forcefully for alternative conceptualizations of their role, and of the role of government in the enforcement of moral and religious teaching.[9] At the same time, the too strident denunciation of Islamic states for the political expression of religious beliefs can also be detrimental. Strategically it would be far more fruitful to recognize the steps made by women living in Islamist and traditionalist states to offer alternative interpretations of their role within Islamic society, and to emphasize the possibility of change.[10] To do otherwise ignores the steps already taken by women and is misleading with respect to changes that have been made: for example, it is widely recognised that women contributed in large numbers to the "protest vote" which secured the election of a relative "moderate," Khatemi, in the 1997 Iranian presidential election.[11] It also risks entrenching conservative interpretations of women's role in the face of blanket external attacks on the integrity of Islamic teaching.

It is not only the reductive and stereotyped language of the press that is attacked by Hite in this section. It is also the use of visual imagery. Picture editors choose photographs that chime with patriarchal conceptions of the need to protect and cherish women. This enables them to dramatize the collapse of political systems that the pictures are intended to document. Rather than raising the profile of women's concerns in post-revolutionary states, or in conditions of civil war, they reinforce the idea of women as passive receptors of outside circumstance, and at the same time diminish and reduce the societies within which such depredations occur.

Hite notes also the inadequate and decontextualized presentation of issues specifically concerning women. Her reference to what she describes as the "trendy" exception of rape in the Bosnian/Serb conflict is telling. Newspapers presented this as a particular and barbarous illustration of the collapse of civilization and the breakdown in human fellow-feeling the former Yugoslavia, a return to the rape and pillage of the long-distant past, a frightening reminder of the brute forces that lay not far from the surface veneer of civilization.

Yet the significance lies deeper than this. Rape and war are images that have been interwined for thousands of years. One has to think only of the English conquest of Ireland, for example. Likewise, in South Asia women have often been the symbol of territory and honour. When India was partitioned at independence in 1947, women on both sides of the new border were abducted and forcibly "married" into communities to which they did not belong. India and Pakistan subsequently agreed to return these women to the country to which they were deemed to belong (the Muslims to Pakistan, the Hindus and Sikhs to

India) but not to send with them any children resulting from these forced relationships, whether or not the women themselves consented.[12] "Political" rape, targeting women as symbolic of national honour, was similarly a feature of the civil war which produced Bangladesh in 1971. These kinds of reactions, of course, only make sense if women are viewed as the bearers and transmitters of cultural identity, and if to "damage" the purity of a nation's women, and ultimately to take possession of them, is seen as being to damage the possibility of cultural reproduction. Rape, therefore, takes its symbolic power in situations of war from the patriarchal account of the cultural importance of women discussed above, and to reduce it to a simple act of aggression and power is to lose its full significance as a political act. Outside the context of war, social and legal responses to rape exemplify the way in which women's rights, even with respect to personal integrity, are often subordinated to the requirements of a social order built on what might be described as a patriarchal system of power. In some societies raped women may be put to death for adultery,[13] in others their rapist may escape punishment by making an offer of marriage.[14] In such contexts the personal act of rape has a clearly political dimension. However, it is but one exemplification of the way in which sexuality and biological difference are used to deny women an equal citizenship with men, to which we will return.

Which Is More Moral—
Religious Fundamentalism or Secularism?

The root of much of this "not seeing," discomfort with seeing, lies in a defensiveness on the part of "secularists." They fear that it is true, that there is something wrong with them, for not being "religious," for being "liberal." In some way, many people fear that the secular West is in fact truly ugly and a-spiritual, has lost its way—and in the backs of their minds, they believe the problem may be a lack of spiritual values.

A worldwide debate is shaping up: which is "better"—democracy and secularism (with religious freedom), or religious fundamentalism? The knee-jerk, automatic answer is that "religious fundamentalism" is "or course" more "moral" and "spiritual." That the West, with its two hundred years of secular democracy, has become corrupt, godless, amoral, a modern Babylon. But I think this is a false analysis.

"Secularism" is not an amoral philosophy: it is a development which took Western culture over two centuries to create, combining the ethics of religious tradition with its own new theories of democracy and equality. The "secular" values of equality and democracy themselves took centuries to develop, and represent the progression of humanity from a strict hierarchical, feudal society to a system in which individuals are respected. This, to me, is deeply spiritual.

Indeed, "secularism" is the most spiritual force in the world today. Why? Because its democratic value system is progressive, aiding in the development of the spiritual life of each person. It encourages tolerance and understanding of others, thus enriching each person's life. Its value system is a vast improvement over the hierarchical medieval system of fundamentalist religion (which said for several centuries that women did not have souls.) Democratic, secular values allow human beings to relate to others, not by trying to dominate them but by creating a harmonious understanding and community with them.

Secularism stresses that no one should be punished for not agreeing with any one particular religious orthodoxy, whereas fundamentalism believes that there is only one real religion. It is less a system of ethics than a system of "faith," in which you must believe in one male god in order to be "saved."

Conversely, "religious fundamentalism" is more a political movement, French writer Bernard Henri Levy notes, than a religious one. Fundamentalism represents the conservative, reactionary wing of Catholicism, Islam and Judaism. There are other, more moderate wings of these religions which are just as religious, "holy."

If there are problems in modern society, this does not mean that secular democracy is the evil culprit. There were problems too when fundamentalism was in power in the Middle Ages. If the secular tradition, predominant for the last two centuries, is currently facing difficulties, under stress, this does not mean we should give up on democracy, rationalism and equality.

In part, a lack of aesthetics on TV and in cities, in their architecture and shopfronts, for example, are fuelling the drive toward appreciating the mysticism and beauty in the Church. People are longing for more beauty in modern daily life.

I believe feminism is a deeply spiritual movement. Far from being shallow, feminism, with its commitment to freedom and equal human rights, is—in my opinion—more spiritual than fundamentalist religion, with its authoritarian belief structure. The values of "women's liberation" (think of the women in Africa who are against performing clitoridectomies on girls, for example) are more ethical and "spiritual" than those of fundamentalism. The basic goal of feminism is its desire to help people, through sponsoring hundreds of battered women's shelters, through making information available to women about their own bodies, information about sexuality, contraception, and reproduction, plus a wealth of other information—through offering a forum for exchanging ideas, and debate. Feminism as a philosophical movement believes there is a way for us to live peaceably together, and is trying to find it.

Fundamentalism principally attacks the rights of women, not men: it is about restricting the freedom of women in society, not men's ability to practice their religion (there is nothing stopping them). The main change when a new fundamentalist regime takes power (for example, in Afghanistan or Iran) is the instigation of new laws controlling women's bodies and freedom of movement.

Fundamentalist attacks on secularism—both Islamic and Western attacks—focus on women (easy targets?). They accuse women today of lacking spirituality (because they are sexual?) They imply that the cause of women's problems with men is that women have "strayed from the right path": male love and approval are there for women who "follow religious teachings." Muddling together various aspects of modern society, Western fundamentalists attack "non-religious" women as if they were the cause of pornography, violence and "the commercialism of modern life." "Middle class career women" are branded as "cold," and as the "impersonal face of a power mad consumer society."

Islamic fundamentalists are fond of pointing to women's dress in the West as a sign of low spiritual awareness and decadence. For them, there is a contradiction between women's sexuality (Western clothes do not cover women's legs, arms and hair), and women's spirituality. But women's "sexual freedom" is not really about clothing; it is about women's right to control and make decisions about their own bodies, sexually and reproductively. Women's autonomy.

The pope (and the Vatican) is the central protagonist of Western fundamentalism. Is the pope's fundamental attitude toward women really as extreme as that of Islamic fundamentalists in Iran, for example? He certainly endorses the double standard of treatment of women, and keeping women out of power. On the other hand, he has never proposed that women be banned from driving cars (as in Saudi Arabia) or that all women wear nun's habits, like the chador. He is similar to Islamic extremists, however, in that he wants to control women's bodies and sexuality, and use them in the service of patriarchal reproductive ideology. This puts him at loggerheads with the movement for women's rights, and indeed, his latest encyclical saying that moral law should be more important than state parliamentary laws put him at loggerheads with democracy and the entire human rights tradition. Of course, what the Pope says is not accepted by large numbers of Catholics.

I believe these debates are part of women's struggle out of centuries of negativity and repression of their sexuality—part of a larger, ongoing and fascinating debate as to how to redefine our sexuality on our own terms, and improve the definition of the erotic, in general. If we don't have our act perfectly together yet, this is hardly a crime. It hardly means that, if we are sexual in a way fundamentalists do not approve of as "politically correct," we are not spiritual and profound as people. (Women are only "profound," in the fundamentalist tradition, when they think of motherhood.)

In fact, it is a very spiritual and profound journey women are making, creating this redefinition. These experiments with sexual expression, this debate, mean women are capable of transforming not only themselves, but also the flawed tradition from which they come, the tradition which said women had no soul, which even burned women who were "politically incorrect" in the Middle Ages, and the tradition that said Eve, because of her sexual curiosity was the cause of all the suffering of humanity!

In this light, women are being very calm and rational, working through the negative stereotypes toward a more positive and valid sexual expression. This will be a real contribution to the society, for which women should be congratulated, not have stones cast at them. Yet many western men fail to see the significance of feminism for them. They sit back passively and watch while dangerous stereotypes are used against women—women's attempts to gain equal rights are ridiculed, women are depicted as sex bimbos and feminists vilified as "man haters" who "deserve whatever they get."

Don't they see? Why do they refuse to accept that women's progress is important for men's (spiritual) progress too? That it represents a positive step forward for the democratic tradition—a necessary step, if that tradition is to survive?

This fight between fundamentalism and progressive human rights represents a New Politics shaping up. The confrontation between authoritarian religion (with its harsh double standard against women) and the democratic tradition (of human rights and free thought, including feminism) will eclipse in importance old "left" and "right" political divisions in the 21st century. It is said that the 1990s New Right (with fundamentalist values) was created when the left (men of liberal persuasion) in the 1980s deserted feminism, despite its being the most vigorous and active new bud in the democratic political tradition, forming a logical progression out of Enlightenment, democratic thought.

The assumption by Western democracies now that "religion" is "sacred" and "not to be questioned," no matter how extremist or politically active, no matter how it attacks the rights of women—could leave space for a world-wide fundamentalism to emerge, subjugating women à la Margaret Atwood's *The Handmaid's Tale*. This would be a great blow to human rights and everything the West has worked and fought for the past two hundred years.

Without the true equality and integration of women in the West, there will not be enough esprit and pride in Western democracy to keep it alive.

Response

In this final part of her lecture, Hite raises a rich variety of points with respect to the weaknesses of liberalism, and the power of feminism to reinvigorate liberal-democracy. She also discusses the distinctive role of sexuality and sexual difference in the construction of female oppression, an aspect of her argument shared particularly by Wolf and le Doeuff. Like Wolf, she insists that any ethical system that is to avoid oppressing women must be capable of permitting women the dignity to express their sexuality in accordance with their own self-definitions and self-understandings.

By focusing on the moral power of feminism, Hite draws out the dominant theme of this lecture series—the distinctive way in which the focus on women throws into sharp relief some of the problems of contemporary political culture in the west with respect to its failure to ensure equal citizenship rights for all both domestically and in foreign policy. For Hite the problem is one of a regressive movement back to an authoritarian religious structure in which women are oppressed and treated as "less than" the full bearers of human rights.[15] Men as well as women are likely to be affected as restrictive moral codes limit the range of debate or even place legal restrictions on the range of acceptable actions. For Hite the generality of this movement constitutes a "new politics."

This stress on the political necessity of feminism was also powerfully evident in the lecture given by Marilyn French, who insisted that only feminism can offer an acceptable moral account of future social organization that accords dignity, respect and rights to women as well as to men. For both Hite and French the identification of a new global politics arises from a recognition of the apparently similar trends in quite distinct states, historically and politically. French, however, while stressing the way in which religious beliefs entrench the relative powerlessness of women, views the world-wide political degeneration rather more as a consequence of the globalization of economic markets and the nation state's consequent inability to control the domestic economy. French stresses that throughout the world (and in part through the pressure of international institutions such as the International Monetary Fund) this has resulted in the liberalization of markets, and the systematic redistribution of power to a smaller and smaller economic elite.

We might remark further that one other effect of these policies and the resulting social fragmentation has been the increasing attractiveness of political movements which sought to order society through other means than state sponsored economic growth and welfare provision. In the west this sort of movement was represented by the new right, while in the Islamic world Islamist parties were able to exploit the uncertainty and sense of failure of post-colonial aspiration to the modern nation state. This might be taken as evidence that liberalism is incoherent, since it generates policies that ultimately undermine the protection of rights. However, both Nussbaum and O'Neill would surely reply, on the basis of the strategies employed in their lectures, that this would be to accept an flawed account of liberalism.

What our lecturers have shown, therefore, is that gender is a category which may radically subvert comfortable assertions about the capacity of the language of rights to include all people, and to incorporate all those aspects of life and social organization which are necessary to the achievement of human dignity for all. The language certainly has limitations with respect to assuring the achievement of equal citizenship in a modern liberal-democratic state. In particular, rights language may fail to deal with the impediments to the enjoyment of rights arising from the social organization of sexual difference.

As Hite reminds us, this analysis has significance for men as well as women because of its engagement with the politics of diversity, and its requirement that equal dignity requires equal respect for our varying needs in the contexts of different sexuality, ethnicity, life-cycle stages, culture and, of course, gender. To say this does not commit us to the camp of the "difference" feminists, or to radical feminist accounts of the structure of power. Rather it requires us to engage with the social grounding of relations of power, and their intersection with supposedly politically neutral accounts of "just" political, social and economic forms of organization. In so doing these lectures require us to step beyond notions of rights, into a more inclusive ethical account of political virtue, and into a substantive dialogue about that which we need as citizens, both women and men, with all of our myriad differences, and in our specific relationships (in their many different forms) with the state.

Notes

1. See United Nations, *The Convention on the Elimination of All Forms of Discrimination Against Women* DPI/993–98035 (New York: U.N., reprinted February 1993). On the arguments over this convention's enforcement see, for example, Hilary Charlesworth, "Women's Rights as Men's Rights," in Julie Peters and Andrea Wolper, eds., *Women's Rights, Human Rights* (New York and London: Routledge, 1995), pp. 103–114.

2. For example, Elisabeth Friedman, "Women's Human Rights: The Emergence of a Movement," in Peters and Wolper, eds., *Women's Rights, Human Rights*, pp. 18–36.

3. See also the comments on the distinction between the public and the private in the introduction above, pp. 3–4.

4. See, for example, Charlotte Bunch, "Transforming Human Rights from a Feminist Perspective," in Peters and Wolper, eds., *Women's Rights, Human Rights*, pp. 11–18.

5. Charlotte Bunch, "The Intolerable Status Quo: Violence Against Women and Girls," *Progress of Nations 1997*, UNICEF. See Ros Coward, "Sign of the Crimes," *The Guardian*, July 1997.

6. Paradoxically, this may have resulted from a confused extension of the embracing of multi-culturalism and difference in the internal policies of liberal-democratic states, to the acceptance of the claim of cultural particularity by the new revolutionary Islamist regimes. Hence the recognition of cultural diversity in their own domestic politics (together with, in all probability, residual imperialist notions of the cultural backwardness of such societies) led to the attribution of cultural homogeneity to Islamic societies. See the discussion of this point by Deniz Kandiyoti, "Reflections on the Politics of Gender in Muslim Societies: From Nairobi to Beijing," in Mahnaz Afkami, ed., *Faith and Freedom: Women's Human Rights in the Muslim World* (London: I. B. Tauris, 1996), p. 28.

7. Rokeya Sakhawat Hossain, ed. and trans. Roushan Jahan, *Sultana's Dream and Selections form the Secluded Ones* (New York: Feminist Press, 1988), pp. 7–19.

8. See, for example, Raga' El-Nimr, "Women in Islamic Law," in Mai Yamani, ed., *Feminism and Islam* (Reading: Ithaca Press, 1996), pp. 87–103.

9. See, for example, Ziba Mir-Hosseini, "Stretching the Limits: A Feminist Reading of the Shari'a in Post Khomeini Iran," in Mai Yamani, ed., *Feminism and Islam*, pp. 285–321.

10. This suggestion parallels the more general claim of Maria Suarez Toro that to increase the success of claims of women's rights on the international agenda, one has to identify and build on the concerns of local woman, "Popularizing Women's Human Rights at the Local Level: A Grassroots Methodology for Setting the International Agenda," in Peters and Wolper, eds., *Women's Rights, Human Rights*, pp. 189–194. This of course fits closely with the approach of Walzer discussed above, p. 6.

11. See, for example, "Iran's Big Shift: A Stunning Protest Vote Gives the Presidency to a Moderate Cleric Who Promises More Freedom," *Time*, 2 June 1997.

12. Urvashi Butalia, "Muslims and Hindus, Men and Women: Communal Stereotypes and the Partition of India," in Tanika Sarkar and Urvashi Butalia, eds., *Women and Right Wing Movements: Indian Experiences* (London: Zed Books, 1995), pp. 58–81.

13. See the discussion of a Bangladeshi case by Charlotte Bunch, "Women's Rights as Human Rights: Toward a Re-Vision of Human Rights," *Human Rights Quarterly* 12 (1990): 486–498, at p. 493.

14. For other examples, see the discussion by Shahla Haeri, "The Politics of Dishonour: Rape and Power in Pakistan," in Afkhami, ed., *Faith and Freedom*, pp. 161–175.

15. It is interesting to note that Islamic countries too saw an advance in the status of women (although only a limited section of society saw the effects) that was rolled back in the face of the rise Islamist movements. See Kandiyoti, "Reflections on the Politics of Gender in Muslim Societies," pp. 21–24.

About the Editor and Contributors

Sarah Ansari is a lecturer in history at Royal Holloway, University of London. She focuses on Muslims in South Asia and is the author of *Sufi Saints and State Power: The Pirs of Sind, 1843–1947*.

Marilyn French writes feminist analyses of politics and morality, as well as literary criticism. She is also a best-selling novelist. Her publications include *The Women's Room; Beyond Power,* and *The War Against Women*. In fall 1998 her memoir, *A Season in Hell,* will be published.

Shere Hite is a cultural historian and researcher, and is the author of *The Hite Report; The Hite Report on Male Sexuality; Women and Love; The Hite Report on the Family; Women as Agents of Revolutionary Change*; and, most recently, *The Hite Report on Hite*.

Alison Jeffries is a lecturer in politics at Royal Holloway, University of London. She writes on ideology and gender as well as on British politics and is working on a book entitled *Parents, Children, and Citizenship*.

Michèle le Doeuff was professor of women's studies at the University of Geneva at the time of the lectures. She now divides her time between Paris and Oxford. She is working on a book about women, knowledge, and power that will be the natural successor volume to her *Hipparchia's Choice*.

Martha Nussbaum is Ernst Freund Professor of Law and Ethics at the University of Chicago, with appointments in the Law School, the Philosophy Department, and the Divinity School. Her most recent books are Cultivating Humanity: A Classical Defense of Reform in Liberal Education (1997) and *Sex and Social Justice* (a collection of essays, 1998). From 1986 to 1996 she was a research adviser at the World Institute for Development Economics Research, Helsinki, a division of the United Nations University.

Onora O'Neill is principal of Newnham College, Cambridge. She has written widely on ethics and political philosophy. Her books include *Faces of Hunger: An Essay on Poverty, Justice, and Development; Constructions of Reason;* and *Towards Justice and Virtue*.

Naomi Wolf writes and lectures on women's issues. She is the author of *The Beauty Myth; Fire with Fire;* and *Promiscuities: A Secret History of Desire*.